Lighthouses
OF THE Great Lakes

Your Guide to the Region's
Historic Lighthouses

Text by Todd R. Berger
Photographs by Daniel E. Dempster

A Pictorial
Discovery Guide

VOYAGEUR PRESS

Edited by Kari Cornell
Designed by Andrea Rud
Printed in China

04   05   06   5   4

Library of Congress Cataloging-in-Publication Data
Berger, Todd R., 1968–
    Lighthouses of the Great Lakes : your guide to the region's historic lighthouses / text by Todd R. Berger ; photographs by Daniel E. Dempster.
        p. cm. — (A pictorial discovery guide)
Includes bibliographical references and index.
    ISBN 0-89658-517-4 (hardcover)
    1. Lighthouses—Great Lakes—Pictorial works. I. Title. II. Series.
    VK1023.3 .B47 2002
    386'.855'0977—dc21
                                            2002004496

Distributed in Canada by Raincoast Books,
9050 Shaughnessy Street, Vancouver, B.C. V6P 6E5

Published by Voyageur Press, Inc.
123 North Second Street, P.O. Box 338
Stillwater, MN 55082 U.S.A.
651-430-2210, fax 651-430-2211
books@voyageurpress.com
www.voyageurpress.com

Educators, fundraisers, premium and gift buyers, publicists, and marketing managers: Looking for creative products and new sales ideas? Voyageur Press books are available at special discounts when purchased in quantities, and special editions can be created to your specifications. For details contact the marketing department at 800-888-9653.

Frontispiece: *The Lighthouse Establishment erected the original lighthouse on New York's Tibbets Point in 1827. The Tibbets Point Light that stands today was built in 1854.*

Title page: *Construction of Wisconsin's Wind Point Light began in 1877. Congress appropriated $100,000 for the project, and the 108-foot tower was first lit on October 6, 1880.*

Title page, inset: *This third-and-a-half-order Fresnel lens remains in the lantern room of the Sodus Point Light along Lake Ontario.*

Dedication page: *Michigan's Au Sable Point Light in Pictured Rocks National Lakeshore was first lit on August 19, 1874.*

Opposite the contents page:
At forty-five feet, the tower at Minnesota's Split Rock Light is quite petite. But the light station's home atop the 130-foot cliff at Stony Point provides a commanding keeper's view over Lake Superior.

Contents page, inset: *The sand dunes along the coast of Lake Michigan can be spied through the portholes of Big Sable Point Light in Michigan.*

Author Dedication

To my 1991 Honda Civic and my right knee.

———○———

Photographer Dedication

To my parents who instilled in me a curiosity of the world, to my wife, Denise, who always keeps me on the right path, and to my children who keep me young at heart.

Contents

Acknowledgments

I would like to thank a few people and institutions that made the writing of this book possible. Michael Dregni, editorial director of Voyageur Press, who had the faith in my abilities to contract me to do this book. Kari Cornell, editor at Voyageur Press, whose insight, suggestions, and patience were appreciated throughout. The librarians at the Minneapolis Public Library, Saint Paul Public Library, and University of Minnesota Libraries for their incredible help in finding source material. My family, especially my mom, who smilingly endured me skipping holiday events so I could write. And finally, I would like to thank the hundreds of volunteers, caretakers, historical society employees, and Coast Guardsmen who helped me gather information about their lighthouses as I traveled around the Great Lakes.

Todd R. Berger

Michigan's Holland Harbor Light is known locally as "Big Red." The gabled-roof pierhead light marks the channel between Lake Macatawa and Lake Michigan.

Photography Acknowledgments

Photographing this book was a labor of love but it wouldn't have been possible without the patience and understanding of my wife, Denise, and my children, Jason and Julia, who put up with my long absences as I worked on this project. While I was on the road Denise had to take over my home duties as well as continue with her own, and I appreciate it more than she could ever know. I would also like to thank my parents, who watched my daughter during the one trip that Denise and I were able to take together. I owe a debt of gratitude to Jonathan Roberts who loaned me his new Nikon shift lens before he'd even had the chance to use it himself. I would like to thank Adam Jones for sharing his digital expertise and for loaning me some specialized Canon equipment until I purchased the Nikon version with a grant from the Indiana Arts Commission and the National Endow-ment for the Arts. Bruce Morris also deserves thanks for pulling strings to get equipment I ordered to me on time. I would also like to thank Cary Bouchard who, even though he had a new baby at home, agreed to fly me around the Apostle Islands so that I could take some aerial photographs.

Traveling the extensive coastline of the Great Lakes was an exhaustive and lonely pursuit, but it was a worth-while trip. I met some truly wonderful people on the road, and I would very much like to thank those who took the time to talk to me while I was waiting out bad weather or waiting for that moment of perfect light. Thank you to the many waiters, waitresses, and towns-people who pointed me in the right direction when I was lost and often advised me of wonderful vantage points in which to capture the lighthouses at their best.

Photographic Notes

The images in this book were captured using Nikon 35mm and Mamiya medium format equipment. I use Nikon F100 and N90s bodies in addition to Nikon lenses rang-ing from 18mm to 500mm. I used a 1.4x teleconvertor on my 500mm lens to achieve an effective focal length of 700mm. I also used perspective control lenses to avoid the keystoning effect that normally occurs in architec-tural photography. When possible, I also used a Mamiya 645 Pro body with lenses from 35mm to 420mm. To achieve the 420mm focal length, I combined a 210mm lens with a 2x teleconvertor. I captured some of the Lake Michigan photos using a Canon 24mm tilt/shift lens on a Canon Elan body. I shot nearly all of the images with the camera mounted on a Gitzo 320 Studex tripod with a Bogen 3039 head.

All of the images in this book were created using Fuji film. I used Fuji Velvia transparency film to create the majority of the images. The Velvia provided the rich, saturated color that I prefer in my landscapes. When I needed a lower contrast film or when people were domi-nant in the image I used Fuji Provia. Some of the light-houses required a bit of a hike, so I carried both me-dium format and 35mm bodies plus an assortment of lenses in a Tenba photo backpack. I used other Tenba bags to store additional equipment when I worked out of my vehicle.

Introduction

The most fearsome Great Lake seemed as treacherous as a farm pond as we prepared to launch our sea kayaks on a beautiful July day. We had been blessed with nonstop sunshine during our four-day paddle among Lake Superior's Apostle Islands off the northern coast of Wisconsin, and the twenty-four-foot, two-person kayaks seemed a little excessive for such calm seas. We could have easily and more comfortably made the two-mile crossing from Oak Island to Raspberry Island in a standard canoe, I thought. But I knew the lake could be very fickle, even among the sheltered islands of the Apostles. Canoes were out of the question for a paddle on the big lake.

Our destination was the Raspberry Island Light, on the southwestern side of the island, one of eight lighthouses on six different islands within the Apostle Islands National Lakeshore. The station was one of the few Great Lakes lighthouses built during the Civil War. Today, the National Park Service opens the lighthouse to visitors willing to make the effort to get to the island by private boat or water taxi.

We were willing, and we launched our sea kayaks from the landing on Oak Island. Wearing wetsuits and kayak skirts, which hung from our shoulders on suspenders, we slipped into the seats and fastened the skirts to the kayak. The skirts would prevent flooding should we roll. My kayaking partner and I soon settled into the increasingly familiar, twisting, left-right-left-right paddling pattern, and the kayak sliced forward. I was in the rear and was responsible for the steering of our craft; keeping the nose of the boat aligned with our Raspberry Island destination was surprisingly difficult. Whenever we veered off course, which was quite often, my partner would turn around and give me a look of grave concern. The trouble I was having was really not that surprising, given I had learned how to steer a sea kayak just the day before. I hoped my partner would realize this and would lighten up.

Despite our snaking route across the channel, we arrived on the Raspberry Island beach in a little over an hour and a half. We stowed our gear and set out on the three-quarter-mile hike through the forest to the lighthouse.

Not far into the woods, we passed a birch tree with what seemed to be a ten-foot-diameter trunk. Despite the familiar peeling white bark, I barely recognized the tree as a birch. I realized I had never before seen an old-growth birch tree. Due to the existence of the Raspberry Island Light, Raspberry Island has never been logged. The whole island was protected as a federal reserve and sat placidly through the logging boom of the 1800s while lumbermen stripped the surrounding islands of their old-growth forests. Trees returned to the other islands, but the spindly saplings found upon them are nothing compared to the giant trees found on Raspberry Island.

Farther down the trail, a stand of evergreens caught our attention, and a discussion of exactly what kind of trees they were escalated into an argument. The argument was settled by a throaty voice coming from the woods, a voice that said, simply, "It's yew." We spun around to see a mustachioed man in the uniform of the old Bureau of Lighthouses. He was sitting on a rock, smoking. Stunned, we didn't say anything for a few seconds. Looking us in the eye and exhaling, he said again, "It's yew."

We regained our composure. "Thanks," I said politely, and we moved on up the trail, not quite sure what to make of the encounter. We looked back a couple of times, and he was still there on his stone, wisps of smoke swirling above his cap. Perhaps Raspberry Island was an

Outer Island Light on Lake Superior is one of eight lighthouses within Wisconsin's Apostle Islands National Lakeshore.

interactive island, where you simply had to voice questions into the forest and strategically placed lighthouse keepers would answer them. Seemed unlikely, but just in case, when we came across a plant of unknown species farther up the trail, I asked in an exaggerated tone, "Hmmmm. What kind of plant is this?" We looked into the trees. No response. A little disappointed, we continued on.

Soon, the forest gave way to a neatly trimmed lawn. We stepped into the sunshine and looked up at Raspberry Island Light—a forty-six-foot, white-sided, square tower rising from the front of a large two-story keeper's house. A red-brick, green-trimmed fog signal building and two outhouses; a combination stairway/tram to the waterline; a brick oil house; a boathouse and a pier; several other outbuildings; and a small garden stood nearby. The station sits on a cliff, overlooking the blue expanse of Lake Superior.

The lighthouse itself is no longer active; its navigational beacon was moved to a steel pole in front of the lighthouse in 1957. Raspberry Island Light's fifth-order Fresnel lens has been removed from the tower and is now displayed at the Madeline Island Historical Society. The National Park Service has since restored the historic building to its 1920s appearance. Today, a park ranger with a wide, flat-brimmed hat and neatly pressed khaki-green uniform greeted us from the back door of the lighthouse. She would be our tour guide.

We followed the ranger into the kitchen. A vintage cookstove stood to one side along with a porcelain sink and cast-iron hand pump connected to cisterns in the basement. The small, tidy kitchen had an air of nineteenth-century simplicity and functionality: I could almost smell the blueberry pie. As we moved our way through the keeper's house, the floorboards creaked; the dwelling had the feeling of a country farmhouse. The ranger led us to the second floor, where we stepped onto the winding stairs that led to the tower. On our own now, we climbed to the lantern room.

From the lantern room, we looked out over Lake Superior toward the Bayfield Peninsula and Raspberry Bay. Pinpoints of bright sunlight sparkled on the water. Sailboats moved slowly between the island and the mainland, taking advantage of the light winds and the glorious sunshine.

* * *

The Raspberry Island Light is but one of 312 American and Canadian light stations standing today among the 94,000 square miles of water and more than 11,000 miles of coastline that make up the Great Lakes. About two hundred of those stations remain active with a navigational beacon in the tower, and many historic lighthouses on the Great Lakes still play a crucial role in guiding ships, even in this age of satellite navigation. Lighthouses have sprouted along the lakes as the shipping patterns have changed, constantly evolving with the times.

Commercial vessels have sailed these lakes since 1679, when the French-Canadian Robert Cavelier, Sieur de la Salle, launched his ship *Le Griffon*. But when *Le Griffon* sailed from Green Bay later that year and vanished beneath the waters of Lake Michigan, it became a harbinger of the hundreds of vessels that would later suffer similar mysterious fates.

Early French ships on the Great Lakes carried beaver pelts, explorers, and missionaries, and by 1700, a fur-trading center was established on Mackinac Island in the straits between Lakes Michigan and Huron. Forts sprung up throughout the region, too. The French were content with their empire based largely on the pursuit of beavers, but the British weren't at all content with France's stronghold in North America. The British formed an alliance with the Iroquois and attacked the French in North America. As a result, what became known as the French and Indian War raged from 1755 until 1763, ending with the signing of the Treaty of Paris. The treaty ceded the Great Lakes and all of French North America to the English victors.

The British were interested in furs as well, and pelts remained the main cargo on the lakes until after the turn of the nineteenth century. When the American Revolution ended in 1783 the southern Canadian boundary was set along and through the Great Lakes, giving all of the lakes but Lake Michigan both American and Canadian shores. After the War of 1812, other treaties would demilitarize the lakes and allow for free access of American, British, and, after Canada became a country in 1867, Canadian ships.

Settlers soon began to venture west along the lakes. Many were immigrants drawn to the region to build canals, log forests, till the fields, and work the mines. Irish, Germans, Swedes, Norwegians, Finns, Swiss, Dutch, Poles, and a smattering of other nationalities took to the lakes in search of steady work and cheap land. On their backs, the future lighthouse cities of Duluth, Milwaukee, and Chicago rose by the waters' edges.

As the fur trade declined in the nineteenth century, entrepreneurs on the Great Lakes first took aim at the

The 1863 Raspberry Island Light in the Apostles is one of only three lighthouses on the Great Lakes built during the Civil War.

Left: *In 1849, the Lighthouse Establishment activated Copper Harbor Light on Lake Superior. The Whitefish Point Light was lit the same year, making the two lighthouses the oldest on the big lake.*

Above: *Dozens of lighthouses on the Great Lakes are open to the public. Some, such as Wisconsin's Raspberry Island Light and Michigan's Au Sable Point Light, pictured here, even have tour guides.*

vast forests. Clear-cutting the old-growth stands of oak, maple, pine, hickory, and birch, they shipped the lumber to markets farther down the lakes. But it was the uncovering of deep veins of ore that would change the face of shipping on the lakes. With the 1844 discovery of a huge vein of iron ore in Michigan's Upper Peninsula, companies and individuals scrambled to the region to mine the ore. The unearthing of copper in 1846 on the Keewenaw Peninsula set off the first full-scale mining rush in U.S. history, as thousands swarmed northward in search of the precious metal. Forty years later, the first trainloads of ore rolled off Minnesota's Iron Range bound for loading docks along the Lake Superior shore.

The ore was shipped over the lakes to the industrial cities of Buffalo, Cleveland, and overland to Pittsburgh, home to iron foundries. The foundries processed the ore, and the resulting iron was then shipped back over the lakes to the manufacturing cities of Detroit, Milwaukee, and Chicago. The finished machine parts, tools, wagons, and ships—and later tractors and cars—then returned to the water, bound for consumers all over the Midwest and the world.

The Great Lakes lay in the agricultural heartland of the United States and British-controlled Canada. After farms developed in the region in the 1800s, the waters played a vital role in getting the diverse products of farmers to cities around the world. Ship holds carried Chicago-butchered meat, Iowa grain, and Wisconsin milk and cheese. As the mining, manufacturing, logging, farming, and shipping industries developed, lighthouses began to appear around the Great Lakes. The navigational beacons helped guide ships safely between ports, playing a vital role in the development of American industry.

* * *

But none of that was on my mind as I looked out over Lake Superior from the Raspberry Island Lighthouse lantern room. On that beautiful summer day, I was imagining what it must have been like to be a lighthouse keeper in the 1800s, smartly dressed in a uniform not unlike that of the smoking keeper we had encountered earlier in the day. I thought about what it would have been like to stand watch at night, scanning Raspberry Bay for ships in trouble. I thought about what it would have been like to watch the great November storms approach from the west from this vantage point high

You can climb to the lantern room of about forty different Great Lakes lighthouses. At many, including Minnesota's Split Rock Light on Lake Superior, the view of the Great Lake on which they stand is extraordinary.

above Lake Superior. I could almost hear the foghorn, and in my mind, I could see the sweep of the light.

I felt the tap of my kayaking partner on my shoulder. "Look," he said, pointing away from the lake toward the forest. Our smoking lightkeeper strolled from the woods and onto the lawn, walking toward the lighthouse. Jolted back to reality, I realized it was time to go anyway, so with one last look out over the lake, we made our way down the tower stairs and left the lighthouse by way of the front porch. As we rounded the back of the lighthouse, we passed the keeper, who was about to lead another tour group into the lighthouse. He was a National Park Service employee enjoying a break in the woods, not a time-traveling lightkeeper who appeared spontaneously to answer our questions. Embarrassed by our naiveté, we silently headed down the trail to our kayaks and paddled back to the modern world.

The skeletal timbers of a ship buried in the Lake Superior sand hint at the treachery ships faced on the lakes. The establishment of lighthouses greatly reduced a ship's chances of suffering a similar fate.

CHAPTER 1

Lighting the Inland Seas

Left: *The Marblehead Light, located at the tip of the Marblehead Peninsula across the bay from Sandusky, Ohio, is the oldest active lighthouse that stands essentially in its original form on the Great Lakes.*

Above: *The winding staircase of the Big Sable Point Light has 130 steps to the lantern room.*

The first lighthouse on the Great Lakes was built in 1781, a signal fire in a lantern room placed on the roof of Fort Niagara at the mouth of the Niagara River. The British established the light after the *HMS Ontario*, a warship loaded with soldiers and war materials sailing from the fort to Oswego, New York, sank in October 1780. A ferocious Halloween gale swept into the region, sending the *Ontario* to the bottom of her namesake lake. More than eighty people on the ship drowned.

The disaster alerted the British, still in the thick of battle with the American colonies, of the need for navigational aids on Lake Ontario to protect their warships. Fort Niagara, a major frontier military garrison that the British had taken over in 1759 during the French and Indian War, seemed an obvious location, and the tower was duly erected.

The British held the fort—and its lighthouse—until 1796, when the military garrison was officially transferred to the United States. The first light on the Great Lakes was soon deactivated; in the early 1800s, the tower at Fort Niagara was torn down. A second, wooden lighthouse went up atop the fort in 1823, but the government replaced it with a sturdy limestone tower that stands today outside the fort at Old Fort Niagara State Park.

The Federal Government Steps In

The Fort Niagara Light didn't last long as a navigational beacon in the hands of the provincial Americans, and it would be awhile before the U.S. government built more Great Lakes lights. The tiny, new nation clinging to the East Coast was poor, remote, and relatively unaware of the value to be gained in expanding its borders westward. However, actions taken by the federal government as early as 1789 would affect the future lights of the Great Lakes and firmly engage the government in Great Lakes lighthouse construction and maintenance.

The ninth act passed by the first American Congress on August 7, 1789, set the stage: "All expenses which shall accrue from and after the 15th day of August, 1789, in the necessary support, maintenance, and repairs of all lighthouses, beacons, buoys, and public piers, erected, placed, or sunk before the passing of this act, at the entrance of or within any bay, inlet, harbor, or port of the United States, for rendering the navigation thereof easy and safe, shall be defrayed out of the Treasury of the United States." The organization created by this act was known as the Lighthouse Establishment. On March 26, 1790, the act was passed again, with an additional clause stating the treasury wouldn't extend funds unless

The current limestone tower at Fort Niagara, which stands just outside the historic fort in Fort Niagara State Park, dates from 1871.

the lighthouses, and the land on which they stood, were transferred to the federal government.

All of the lighthouses built in the colonies before 1789 were erected by state and local governments and were maintained through the collection of fees from vessels sailing into and out of these lighted ports. With the passage of the act, state and local governments slowly began to transfer control of their beacons to the federal government. By 1797, all lighthouses were in Uncle Sam's hands. A few lighthouses were under construction in 1789, and after the passage of the law, they were completed by the federal government. Every newly constructed lighthouse thereafter, including every American lighthouse built on the Great Lakes, was paid for by the federal government.

The highest government officials monitored United States lighthouse construction and maintenance. At first, Secretary of the Treasury Alexander Hamilton was in charge of the lighthouse system, and decisions about lighthouse construction contracts and personnel were even made by the first three presidents, George Washington, John Adams, and Thomas Jefferson. President Washington, in particular, was very interested in expanding America's lighthouse system, believing the United States would inevitably become a world maritime power, and the establishment of lighthouses would help guide America toward this destiny.

The British established the first lighthouse on the Great Lakes at Fort Niagara, New York, in 1781.

Despite such lofty support, the Lighthouse Establishment entered a wayward period after 1792. That year, supervision of the Lighthouse Establishment passed from Secretary Hamilton to the collector of revenue, only to be transferred back to the secretary of the treasury ten years later. In 1813, Secretary of the Treasury Albert Gallatin handed the Lighthouse Establishment back to the collector of revenue, who relinquished control to the Treasury Department yet again in 1820.

As the federal government played a game of hot potato with the Lighthouse Establishment, lighthouses continued to be built. In 1789, only twelve lighthouses stood on American soil. By 1820, that number had jumped to fifty-five. The first lighthouses on the Great Lakes were built during this time.

The First U.S. Lights on the Lakes

After the Fort Niagara Light was darkened in 1796, it took more than twenty years for the American government to turn their attention to building lighthouses on the Great Lakes. The British, who controlled Canada, established two more lighthouses on the Great Lakes after Fort Niagara Light was closed down. In 1804, the British erected a light at Fort Mississauga (later renamed Fort George) on the opposite bank of the Niagara River, and, in 1808, they built the Gibraltar Point Light at York (later renamed Toronto). The Fort Mississauga Light was only active for ten years before it was torn down. Gibraltar Point Light, the oldest remaining lighthouse on the Great Lakes, still stands but is no longer active. As the United States started to move westward into new territories, American lighthouses began to rise along the lakes. The first American lighthouses on the Great Lakes were constructed on Lake Erie in 1818 at Buffalo, New York, and Erie, Pennsylvania. Both were lit for the first time in 1819.

A lighthouse had been planned for the port of Buffalo as early as 1805, but government officials refused to appropriate funds for a beacon. The ensuing War of 1812—which lasted three years—further delayed matters. After the war, funds were finally made available, and the thirty-foot, stone Buffalo Main Light was erected.

The Buffalo Main Light, established in 1819, was one of the first two American lighthouses built on the Great Lakes. The current limestone tower, built in 1833, looks well prepared to stand another 170 years.

The American government established the Erie Land Light in Erie, Pennsylvania, in 1819. It was one of the first two American lighthouses built on the Great Lakes.

Right: *This bivalve fourth-order Fresnel lens was originally installed at Marblehead Light in 1903. Today, the lens is on display at the Marblehead Coast Guard Station near the lighthouse.*

The whitewashed, woodframe keeper's house of the Marblehead Light is surrounded by a Tom Sawyer–esque picket fence.

The original, primitive Marquette Harbor Light on Lake Superior in Upper Michigan dates from 1853. The present lighthouse, completed in 1869, has three-foot-thick basement walls and a solid brick construction, features well suited to weathering any Lake Superior storm.

The original light stood for fifteen years before it was replaced in 1833 by the still-standing sixty-foot limestone tower. After the opening of the Erie Canal in 1825, the new tower was necessary, as shipping traffic in the Buffalo area increased dramatically.

When it was first built, the Erie Land Light was known as the Presque Isle Light. Unbeknownst to the engineers building the lighthouse, a layer of quicksand lurked deep beneath the construction site. Over time, the lighthouse sank. It was rebuilt in 1857, but that tower also sank, this time much more quickly. When the tower that still stands was erected in 1867, engineers shored up the foundation and positioned the lighthouse to keep it from being slowly digested by the earth once again.

From this initial foothold on the shores of Lake Erie, lighthouses sprouted all over the lakes. The first American Lake Ontario lighthouse rose in 1820 on Galloo Island, fifteen miles west of Sackets Harbor, New York. The Galloo Island Light still stands and remains active, though the original tower was shortened by eleven feet in 1867 to better distinguish it from other nearby aids to navigation. Additional early Lake Ontario lights were established at Oswego (1822); Charlotte, which is today part of Rochester, and Rochester Harbor (both 1822); and Sodus Point (1825).

Several other early lighthouses were built on Lake Erie. The Marblehead Light, near Sandusky, Ohio, was established in 1821. Today, Marblehead is the oldest active Great Lakes lighthouse standing essentially in its original form. The Old Fairport Main (Grand River) Light in Fairport, Ohio, was erected in 1825, followed by the Cleveland Light in 1829, which no longer stands, and a light at Portland Harbor, New York, in 1829, a town later renamed Barcelona.

The first lighthouse on Lake Huron was established at Fort Gratiot near the Michigan town of Port Huron in 1825. The Fort Gratiot Light at the head of the St. Clair River was rebuilt just a few years later but remains an active navigational beacon and U.S. Coast Guard Station. The lighthouse in northern Lake Huron near the Straits of Mackinac went up in 1829. The Bois Blanc Island Light was blown over in a strong storm just eight years later, but it was subsequently rebuilt. Another early Lake Huron lighthouse was established in 1832 on Thunder Bay Island off Alpena, Michigan. The tower still stands, although it has been heightened.

The first lighthouse on Lake Michigan was the Chicago Harbor Light, established in 1832. Other early Lake Michigan lights include Michigan's St. Joseph Light, built in 1832; the Old Michigan City Light, built in Indiana in 1837; the Potawatomi Light built in 1838 on Rock Island off Wisconsin's Door Peninsula; and the South Manitou Island Light built in Michigan in 1839. South Manitou Island Light is now part of Sleeping Bear Dunes National Lakeshore. In 1832, the first lightship on the Great Lakes was also established on Lake Michigan at Waugoshance Shoal seventeen miles west of Mackinaw City. The lightship, the *Louis McLane*, was replaced in 1851 by the first offshore reef lighthouse built on the Great Lakes, the Waugoshance Light.

Lake Superior was the last of the Great Lakes to receive aids to navigation. Before the construction of the St. Mary's Falls Ship Canal (the Soo Locks) at Sault Ste. Marie in 1855, all cargo and even some ships traveling between Lake Superior and Lake Huron had to be portaged around the St. Mary's Falls. This portage greatly limited shipping traffic on Lake Superior and thus also limited the need for lighthouses. Despite this, the first lighthouses on Lake Superior predate the locks by six years. The Copper Harbor Light on the Keewenaw Peninsula and the Whitefish Point Light on the approach to the St. Mary's River were both erected in 1849. Other early Lake Superior lights rose off the tip of the Keewenaw Peninsula: Manitou Island Light was built in 1850, and the Marquette Harbor Light was built in 1853. Both of these lighthouses remain active today although they have been rebuilt. Once the Soo Locks were completed, lighthouses sprang up all over the lake.

Fueling the Light

The ancestors of the Midwestern beacons lie in the eastern Mediterranean Sea and predate the Great Lakes lights by as much as 2,800 years—perhaps much longer. These first beacons used wood to fuel their signal lights. By the 1600s, keepers started to replace the wood signal fires with coal-fired beacons. Coal burned much slower and brighter than wood. As with the wood fires, the coal fires required constant vigilance. Keepers had to keep the lantern glass clean and make sure the fires burned bright enough to be seen.

Around the time coal became common in lighthouses, some lighthouse keepers used tallow candles to light the beacons. Some early British lights, including the famed Eddystone Light off the southern coast of

WILLIAM HART'S EXPERIMENT

*n 1825, the idea of lighting a town, much less a lighthouse, with natural gas was met with due skepticism in western New York. But Fredonia gunsmith and entrepreneur William Hart wasn't a skeptic by nature; his spirit was ruled by optimism—with a healthy dash of greed.

The area around Fredonia, just inland from Lake Erie near Dunkirk, was rich in natural gas deposits. Hart thought it might be possible to reap a healthy profit by tapping into that supply, piping the gas into town, and then selling it to residents and shopkeepers. Hart recruited a couple local businessmen to help him with the dirty work, and the entrepreneurs capped some springs and funneled the gas into pipes snaking toward town. Fredonians embraced Hart's initiative, and before long, the town's main streets, shops, and homes were lit under lamps fueled with Hart's natural gas.

However, Hart was hardly a man to sit around and watch the flickering flames of his accomplishments. When Secretary of the Treasury Richard Rush appropriated $5,000 from Congress in 1828 to build a lighthouse at Portland Harbor (later renamed Barcelona) less than twenty miles west of Fredonia, Hart turned his thoughts to the possibility of finding similar gas deposits near the lighthouse to fuel the beacon—all for a handsome profit courtesy of Uncle Sam, of course. It wasn't long at all before Hart could be seen tromping around the woods and meadows near Portland Harbor in search of natural gas.

The Barcelona Light, a rugged-looking fieldstone tower with a keeper's house overlooking the then-busy Portland Harbor, was completed in 1829. As with most American lights of its era, the Barcelona Light initially lit its thirteen Argand lamps with sperm whale oil. The first keeper of the light, retired preacher Joshua Lane, assumed his post on June 1, 1829.

Before long, William Hart introduced himself to Keeper Lane. Hart, like all successful entrepreneurs, had a persuasive manner, and soon the keeper was singing the praises of lighting the tower with natural gas. After all, carrying barrels of whale oil up the circular wooden steps of the forty-foot tower was no picnic for the elderly Lane. So Lane took Hart's idea to use natural gas to the Lighthouse Establishment, and the preacher, who himself possessed considerable persuasive power, convinced the government to back the plan.

With federal greenbacks in his pocket, Hart located a natural gas spring about three-quarters of a mile from the

The fieldstone tower of the Barcelona Light in Barcelona, New York, stands today much as it did when built in 1829. The Lighthouse Board deactivated the station in 1859, and today the tower and the nearby keeper's house are privately owned.

tower, capped the deposit, and funneled the fuel into piping. The pipes led to the base of the tower and then up to the lantern room. In 1830, the Barcelona Light became the first lighthouse in the world lit by natural gas.

The gas-fueled beacon was quite bright, and the uniqueness of the lighthouse was not lost on Keeper Lane. He wrote: "This is one of the greatest natural, philosophical, and mechanical curiosities which the country can produce. As a light for a lighthouse it exceeds, both in quantity and in brilliancy, anything of the kind I ever saw."

But the Barcelona Light and its unique fuel system were not destined to function forever. By 1838, the natural gas spring ran dry, and the lighthouse was converted back to whale oil. In 1844, an October gale slammed into Portland Harbor and demolished much of the bustling lakeport's infrastructure. The lighthouse survived, but the town would never recover as a trade center. Then, in 1852, the nearby town of Westfield established a rail link that diverted freight away from Portland Harbor. Seven years later, the Lighthouse Establishment deactivated Barcelona Light.

The Barcelona Light still stands, and today it even shines, lit by a decorative gas beacon. The privately owned lighthouse is one of the oldest stations standing in its original form on the Great Lakes. The National Historic Landmark sits quietly today, not hinting at its unique history among American lighthouses.

England, were lit with tallow candles initially, as was the first North American lighthouse, Boston Light in Boston Harbor.

Most lighthouses in America first lit before the 1850s, including nearly all of the antebellum Great Lakes lights, were fueled by sperm whale oil. Whale oil burned evenly with a very bright light, qualities perfectly suited to lighthouse duty. And whale oil seemed plentiful. It was hard to imagine ever running low on the fuel, given the size of an individual sperm whale and the huge pods of them that swam off the Atlantic coast.

But by the 1850s, whalers had hunted sperm whales to near extinction, and the supply of the oil did indeed run low. Between 1840 and 1855, the shortage of whales led to a four-fold increase in the price per gallon of whale oil. The federal government soon began a search for a fuel to replace it, luckily for the sperm whale.

In the 1850s, the government conducted tests on numerous fuels, including shark, porpoise, fish, olive, seal, lard, and colza (rapeseed) oils, as well as kerosene (commonly called mineral oil), and natural gas, which had been used successfully at New York's Barcelona Light as early as 1830. Colza oil, common in French lighthouses of the day, initially seemed the best choice, as it was cheap and worked as well as whale oil. However, colza oil is produced from wild cabbage, a plant not common in the United States. Despite the initial enthusiasm, it soon became apparent that there wasn't nearly enough colza oil to supply the nation's lighthouses.

For a while, lighthouse keepers burned lard oil, which was readily available and burned well when first heated to very high temperatures. But by 1878, lighthouse officials had determined that mineral oil was the best option, despite reporting to Congress in 1877 that the fuel "gives off a vapor which, when mingled in a certain proportion with atmospheric air, is capable of exploding with the violence of gunpowder; and the material itself, when once kindled, burns with an energy almost uncontrollable." Even though it was highly explosive,

Right, top: *The Lighthouse Board began to fuel lighthouses with explosive mineral oil around 1877. Though separate oil houses were mandated for storage of the fuel, many lighthouses did not have oil houses until much later. This is the oil house door at Big Bay Point Light, built in 1896.*

Right, bottom: *Since its establishment in 1827, the Tibbets Point Light at Cape Vincent, New York, has been fueled by everything from sperm whale oil to electricity.*

The Wind Point Light near Racine, Wisconsin, was originally lit with kerosene, which was then called mineral oil. Mineral oil was the dominant lighthouse fuel when the Lighthouse Board established this light in 1880.

mineral oil was half the cost of lard oil, so mineral oil it would be. By 1885, mineral oil was the dominant fuel in use across the Great Lakes.

The government also mandated oil rooms or separate oil houses to store the highly flammable fuel, although the government didn't build such oil houses at the light stations on the Great Lakes for many years to come. Before oil houses were built, keepers stored the kerosene in the basement below the keeper's quarters, which didn't sit well with many keepers, particularly those with families sleeping upstairs. When the government finally built the oil houses, the most common style on the Great Lakes was a round, iron building with a pointy top. Though kerosene is no longer used as a lighthouse fuel, the original oil houses still stand at many Great Lakes lights, including Thirty Mile Point Light and Dunkirk Light in New York and Michigan's Pointe Aux Barques Light.

Lamps and Lenses

As with lighthouse fuels, the lamps and lenses used to burn the fuel and intensify the light evolved to become more efficient and effective. As early as the 1720s and 1730s, France and Sweden experimented with reflectors to intensify lighthouses lit by tallow candles. But the first revolution in lighthouse lighting systems came in 1763, when Englishman William Hutchinson invented a catoptric (reflecting) system.

Hutchinson had watched a demonstration where a candle placed inside a reflector-lined wooden bowl produced enough light to read a newspaper two hundred feet away. Hutchinson took the idea and refined it, placing the light source inside a parabolic reflector, a precise bowl-shaped device, which reflected the light into a cone to create a concentrated beam. His catoptric system had useful implications for lighthouses, but the system needed a more powerful light source than tallow candles to be effective.

Around 1780, the Swiss inventor Aimé Argand developed just such a light source. The Argand burner, as it became known, was an oil lamp with a circular, hollow wick. Oxygen passed inside and outside of the wick to produce a more brilliant, nearly smokeless, light. The first Argand burners generated the light of about seven tallow candles, though later designs, which incorporated several refined lamps, produced candlepower in the hundreds. The Hutchinson reflector and the Argand burner found widespread use in Europe after 1789.

The original fourth-order Fresnel lens remains active in the tower of the Forty Mile Point Light on Michigan's Lake Huron shore.

At the same time, the first spider lamp was developed and installed at Boston Light. The lamps consisted of a pan of whale oil with four flat wicks. Though the spider lamps generated acrid fumes and lots of smoke, which prohibited keepers from remaining in the lantern room for an extended period of time, they were the dominant lighting apparatus in U.S. lighthouses until 1812.

In 1807, Winslow Lewis, an American former merchant captain, began experiments to develop a "reflecting and magnifying lantern." By 1810, Lewis secured a patent for his device, which "incorporated" the work of several earlier inventors. Lewis's "invention" included a lamp similar to Argand's, a parabolic reflector similar to Hutchinson's, and a green glass lens placed in front of the light beam, similar to a lens English glasscutter Thomas Rogers had invented in 1789.

In the summer of 1810, with Henry Dearborn, collector of customs in Boston, present, Lewis tested his

The 1854 tower at Tibbets Point, built of brick and coated with stucco, remains active today. The original fourth-order Fresnel lens, put in place during the 1854 reconstruction, remains in the lantern room.

purloined apparatus in one of the towers at the Thacher Island (Cape Ann) Light in Massachusetts. Dearborn was impressed, as the system produced a much brighter light than the spider lamps and used only about half as much fuel. Dearborn recommended to Secretary of the Treasury Albert Gallatin that all lighthouses in the United States be outfitted with the Lewis lamp. Gallatin agreed and appealed to Congress to buy Lewis's patent, to pay him to install the lamp in all U.S. lighthouses, and to pay him to maintain the lighthouses for seven years. In 1812, Congress appropriated $60,000 toward this goal, and by 1815, all American lighthouses had the Lewis lamp.

For nearly forty years, the Lewis lamp was the domi-nant lighting apparatus in U.S. lighthouses, including every station built on the Great Lakes before 1852. But while the Lighthouse Establishment stuck by Winslow Lewis's device, the Europeans were using a vastly supe-rior lighting apparatus, the Fresnel lens, which was first tested in 1822 and was thereafter quickly installed in most European lighthouses.

The Fresnel Lens

Augustin Fresnel, an engineer working on roads and canals for the French government, developed his remark-able namesake lens in his spare time. Fascinated by ge-ometry, mathematics, and the elements of light, he took a look at existing lighting systems, such as the catoptric

Left: *Minnesota's Split Rock Light on Lake Superior, completed in 1910, is one of the few towers on the Great Lakes that still contain a working mercury-float clockwork turning mechanism. At Split Rock, the turning mechanism supports a beautiful third-order bivalve Fresnel lens.*

Above: *At the Pointe Aux Barques Life-Saving Station visitors can view the dismantled parts of a Fresnel lens.*

(reflecting) apparatus developed by Hutchinson. He found the reflecting system allowed considerable light to escape from the top and sides of the apparatus, which diminished the beacon's strength. Fresnel also examined the dioptric (refracting) system, which was developed after Hutchinson and included a refracting lens that bent the stray light and directed it back toward the main beam. Though an improvement, the dioptric system still allowed considerable light to escape.

Fresnel's solution was a catadioptric lens, which combined both methods. A light source was surrounded by prismatic rings of glass, each cut to a different, mathematically precise angle. The prisms reflected and refracted most light that strayed from its proper plane, directing it back to become parallel with the main beam of light, intensifying that beam. The beam then passed through a central magnifying bull's-eye lens, which further intensified the light and projected it out in a brilliant, concentrated sheet from the light station.

Over time, another advantage of the Fresnel lens became apparent: It could be easily altered to provide distinctive light characteristics, allowing mariners to distinguish not only between closely placed lighthouses but between a lighthouse and other shore lights. The lens could be fixed, or stationary; flashing, or rotating; or a combination thereof, producing an easily recognizable beacon. Colored screens could also be placed inside the lens to further distinguish the light or to mark specific hazards.

A flashing light was created by rotating the Fresnel lens at a constant speed and allowing the light source to pass behind brass panels, creating a precise period of light followed by a precise period of darkness. The lens rotated using a clockwork mechanism, similar to a grandfather clock with weights hanging from cables running the height of the tower. Keepers needed to wind the clockwork mechanism several times during a night's watch. At first, the lens apparatus rotated on wheels, and later on ball bearings, but with the invention of the mercury float system in 1890, lenses rested on a pool of mercury which allowed for much smoother and faster revolutions of the lenses.

Unfortunately, not many of these turning mechanisms survive in Great Lakes light towers today. Split Rock Light in Minnesota, though inactive, contains one of the few functioning mercury-float clockwork turning mechanisms remaining in a Great Lakes lighthouse. Beacons still rotate, of course, but their systems are powered by electricity.

There were seven orders, or sizes, of Fresnel lenses, categorized in descending order. The first-order lens is twelve feet tall and measures thirty-six inches from the light source to the glass of the lens, a measurement known as focal length. The smallest lens, the sixth order, is about two feet tall and has a focal length of 5.9 inches. There is also a third-and-a-half-order Fresnel lens squeezed in between the third- and fourth-order lenses bringing the total number of lens orders to seven. Six orders of Fresnel lenses found use on the Great Lakes; only the first-order lens never saw service on the lakes as its luminous range, the distance at which a lighthouse beacon can be seen, was more powerful than was necessary on the inland waters. In fact, very few second-order lenses were placed in Great Lakes lights, including the Rock of Ages Light off Isle Royale in Lake Superior, White Shoal Light east of the Straits of Mackinac, and the Spectacle Reef Light in northern Lake Huron.

Many Fresnel lenses, put in place as long ago as 150 years, remain in use in Great Lakes lighthouses today. Their remainder is a testament to the sophistication and effectiveness of the lens. But despite the vastly superior lens technology available in Europe, the American Lighthouse Establishment almost totally ignored the Fresnel lens for thirty years after it was first tested. On the Great Lakes, not a single lighthouse received a Fresnel lens before the 1850s.

Stephen Pleasonton

Stephen Pleasonton, Fifth Auditor of the Treasury and Superintendent of Lighthouses beginning in 1820, carries much of the blame for America's glacial response to the development of the Fresnel lens. Pleasonton was an accountant with no experience in either maritime navigation or lighthouse engineering. His primary concern was keeping costs in the Lighthouse Establishment at a bare-bones minimum. He did this at the expense of quality construction, lighthouse effectiveness, and light station safety. He relied heavily on the advice of Winslow Lewis, the man who had installed his lighting apparatus in U.S. lighthouses a few years before Pleasonton took office. The connection between these two men bordered on corrupt, and American lighthouses, as well as the mariners who relied on them, paid the price—they were forced to use crudely inferior lighting technology while Fresnel lenses in European lighthouses blazed away.

Under Pleasonton, Lewis became the primary builder of the lighthouses themselves. Pleasonton would consult Lewis regarding a bid to build a lighthouse, Lewis would declare the bid too high, Pleasonton would reject the higher bid, Lewis would make a lower bid, and finally Pleasonton would award him the contract. Lewis would then have the lighthouse constructed within the constraints of a too-low budget, resulting in many structurally unsound lighthouses rising across the Great Lakes, as well as across the country.

Some of Lewis's lighthouses didn't last long. Michigan's Fort Gratiot Light, built in 1825, toppled a mere four years after construction. The original Chicago Harbor Light, built in 1831, collapsed just hours after the last laborer had set down his tools. The station wasn't officially activated until 1832 after it had been rebuilt. In fact, nearly every Great Lakes light erected before 1852, during the time Lewis was building lighthouses, has been rebuilt at least once. Great Lakes lighthouses standing in their original forms, such as the 1821 Marblehead Light in Ohio and the 1829 Barcelona Light in New York, are true historical gems.

Pleasonton and Lewis maintained their symbiotic relationship for some time, though not without criticism. By the 1830s, ship captains were reporting that the lighthouses of the United States were significantly dimmer than the navigational beacons of Europe. In 1837, Edmund M. and George W. Blunt, the publishers of the magazine the *American Coast Pilot*, launched a scathing attack on the Lighthouse Establishment, contending that American lighthouse construction was generally shoddy and that the light cast by Lewis's lamps was grossly inadequate.

Congress responded to the Blunts' criticisms in several ways. Commodore Matthew C. Perry traveled overseas to inspect European lighthouses and to acquire two Fresnel lenses. Congress also divided the country's lighthouses up into eight regional districts, with two on the Great Lakes (the boundary between these two districts was at the Detroit River entrance to Lake Erie). Congress assigned a naval officer to each district to inspect all district lighthouses and review operations. The ensuing inspection reports, as well as Perry's report upon his return from Europe, supported the Blunts' criticisms.

Despite overwhelming evidence that the American lighthouse system needed revamping, Congress did little to improve the situation. Beginning in 1842, the House Committee on Commerce examined lighthouse expenditures dating back to 1816. Despite the negative inspection reports of four years earlier and despite the fact that the two Fresnel lenses that Perry brought back from

The Grand Traverse (Cat's Head) Light on Michigan's western coast was one of the last Great Lakes lighthouses built before the Lighthouse Board took over the administration of lighthouses. First lit in 1853, it had to be replaced just five years later.

Europe had since been installed in the twin towers of New Jersey's Navesink Light to widespread praise, the Committee gave the Lighthouse Establishment and Stephen Pleasonton a generally positive review.

The criticism from other sources, however, continued. In 1842, Secretary of the Treasury Walter Forward appointed I. W. P. Lewis, a civil engineer and a nephew of Winslow Lewis, as a special agent to inspect lighthouses. Following an inspection tour in New England, the younger Lewis not only reiterated the earlier criticisms of the poor construction and inferior lighting, but also publicly accused his uncle of incorporating previously patented designs in the making of his lighting apparatus.

Pleasonton responded that I. W. P. Lewis's report misrepresented the truth, and he characteristically stressed that his lighthouses were routinely built at great cost savings to the government, a fact that likely influenced the House Committee on Commerce's report on lighthouse expenditures. Winslow Lewis also responded, calling his nephew unqualified to make such a report and saying the report was almost completely inaccurate from top to bottom, including the accusation of him stealing the idea for his lighting apparatus. As it happened, the assurances of these two powerful men were enough to maintain the status quo: Neither Congress nor the Secretary of the Treasury took any further action on the matter in 1842.

Above: *Congress appropriated funds to build Michigan's Big Sable Point Light in 1856, but the lighthouse wasn't completed until after the Civil War.*

Left: *The Little Sable Point Light towers over the beach at Silver Lake State Park on Michigan's western coast. The lantern room still contains the original, 1874 third-order Fresnel lens.*

THE MISTAKEN LIGHTHOUSE OF MICHIGAN ISLAND

The town of La Pointe, on Madeline Island in the southern part of Wisconsin's spectacular Apostle Islands archipelago, was a booming fur-trading town in the mid 1800s. In fact, La Pointe was the busiest port on all of Lake Superior. After the St. Mary's Falls Ship Canal (the Soo Locks) at Sault Ste. Marie opened in 1855 and shipping became big business on the lake, it only made sense that a lighthouse be built to guide vessels into the bustling harbor at La Pointe.

Congress appropriated funds and the Lighthouse Board hired a contractor. In Milwaukee a crew of thirty-eight men boarded a ship loaded with construction materials and sailed through the new Soo Locks and on to La Pointe. Accounts differ about what happened next. As best as can be determined, the contractor and his crew met the local collector of customs at La Pointe for instructions on precisely where to build the lighthouse.

Well, the collector of customs hadn't heard anything about the building of a lighthouse—the arrival of the contractor and his crew came as a complete surprise. After a little bit of head scratching, the collector of customs instructed the contractor to build the lighthouse on the southeastern end of Michigan Island, seventeen miles northeast of La Pointe. So the contractor checked the coordinates on his map, rounded up his men, and set sail for Michigan Island.

At Michigan Island, the contractor surveyed the site and settled on a spot for the lighthouse. The southeastern end of Michigan Island is bordered by a 110-foot sandstone cliff, but the crew wasn't daunted by the formidable obstacle, though the workers spent several days hauling supplies and equipment up the bluff. Construction commenced immediately, and it wasn't long before the crew completed the quaint whitewashed stone tower and attached two-story keeper's house. The lighthouse was lit for the first time in the spring of 1857.

After the work was completed, the contractor dutifully notified the Lighthouse Board, fully expecting payment for his work and materials. It must have been quite a shock when he learned that the lighthouse should have been built on the north shore of Long Island just south of La Pointe. Unless the contractor built a lighthouse in the proper location, the Lighthouse Board would not pay the contractor.

Making the most of a difficult situation, the contractor figured payment for one lighthouse was better than no payment, so in 1858 he acquired supplies and rounded up his men once again, and they built the La Pointe Light on Long Island. When it was done he finally received payment for materials and construction of the second lighthouse, and undoubtedly the contractor washed his hands of lighthouse work.

The Lighthouse Board operated the Michigan Island Light through the 1857 shipping season and then deactivated it. Workers removed the lantern room and shipped it to Detroit, where it became the lantern room for the rebuilt lighthouse at Windmill Point on Lake St. Clair in 1866.

In 1869, however, the government decided the Michigan Island Light would be useful for ships approaching La Pointe and the growing city of Ashland, Wisconsin, from the east. The Lighthouse Board spent $6,000 to build a new lantern room and shape up the now-dilapidated station. The sixty-four-foot tower would remain active until 1929 when the government decided a taller lighthouse was needed. The Bureau of Lighthouses hired a contractor to build a second, 112-foot light tower and adjacent keeper's house one hundred feet from the original station.

The Michigan Island Old (First) Light, as it is officially known, remains standing, preserved by the National Park Service within the Apostle Islands National Lakeshore. To visit the station, travel to Michigan Island by water taxi or private boat—just make sure to get off on the correct island.

The Lighthouse Board

By 1851, the protests against the American lighthouse system had crescendoed, forcing Congress to act. In March 1851, Congress ordered Secretary of the Treasury Thomas Corwin to investigate the operations of the Lighthouse Establishment. Corwin formed an investigative board comprised of two senior naval officers, one junior naval officer, two army engineers, and a civilian scientist, to review all matters related to the American lighthouse system.

In January 1852, the Corwin board issued a mammoth 760-page report that found little of value in Stephen Pleasonton's Lighthouse Establishment. The report unequivocally supported the adoption of the Fresnel lighting system, calling it "greatly superior to any other mode of light-house illumination, and in point of economy is nearly four times as advantageous as the best system of reflectors and . . . lamps." According to the report, the Lewis lamps in use were poorly made and not sufficiently ventilated, the quality of the whale oil was inferior, the reflectors were "defective in form, materials, and finish," and the keepers lacked basic instruction on how to tend the lighting system under their watch. The report also strongly criticized the use of Tripoli powder, an abrasive cleanser designed for brass and copper, which was used to clean the silver reflectors; the harsh cleanser removed the delicate reflective silver coating after only a few scrubbings. The Corwin board report did not mince words in stating "the illuminating apparatus in the United States is of a description now nearly obsolete throughout all maritime countries." Further, the board made extensive recommendations for the complete revamping of the Lighthouse Establishment.

In October 1852, after fifteen years of inaction, the U.S. Congress ousted Stephen Pleasonton and abolished the Lighthouse Establishment. In its place they created the Lighthouse Board based on the recommendations of Secretary Corwin's investigative board. The Lighthouse Board consisted of nine members, including officials in similar positions to those on the investigative board, as well as another member from the Army Corps of Engineers, an additional civilian scientist, and the Secretary of the Treasury himself, who would be ex-officio president of the Board.

The Lighthouse Board wasted no time in installing Fresnel lenses in American lighthouses. All new lighthouses built after 1852 had a Fresnel lens, and by 1859, all existing American lighthouses had the lenses. The lenses proved their value almost immediately. They ef-

fectively doubled the luminous range of the beacons and used only one quarter the fuel of Winslow Lewis's apparatus.

The Lighthouse Board immediately recognized the need for detailed instructions for lightkeepers, who during the Pleasonton era often had little training and limited written instructions on how to operate and maintain a light station. Officially, each light station was to post a list of printed instructions in the lighthouse, but the inspections of 1851 determined that few lighthouses complied. In 1852, the Board issued the first edition of *Instructions and Directions for Light-House and Light-Vessel Keepers of the United States.* The instructions included not only specific directions, parts lists, and diagrams for the lighting equipment, but also numerous rules for the keepers, ranging from no drinking liquor while on duty to maintaining "the utmost neatness of buildings and premises."

The Lighthouse Board also greatly improved the information available to mariners about light characteristics. The first light list was published by Winslow Lewis back in 1817, and Pleasonton's Lighthouse Establishment published their *List of Lighthouses, Beacons and Floating Lights of the United States* in 1838, but neither list placed a premium on accuracy and both were poorly organized, making them of little value to mariners. The Lighthouse Board issued a considerably more accurate and easier to use *Light List* in 1852, and beginning in 1869, the list was revised annually.

The Lighthouse Board also began a long-overdue reconstruction of American lighthouses at this time. Construction crews tore down and rebuilt numerous substandard, Winslow Lewis–era lighthouses. On the Great Lakes, the board rebuilt New York's Tibbetts Point Light in 1854, the Grand Traverse (Cat's Head) Light on Lake Michigan in 1858, and the Manitou Island Light on Lake Superior in 1861. In all, dozens of Great Lakes lights were rebuilt during the early years of the Lighthouse Board.

However, lighthouse construction ground to a halt with the outbreak of the Civil War. Between 1861 and 1865, only six lighthouses were built or rebuilt on the Great Lakes, including the rebuilding of the Whitefish Point Light in Michigan in 1861 and the construction of the Raspberry Island Light in Wisconsin's Apostle Islands in 1863. Plans to build other lighthouses were simply delayed. As early as 1856, Congress appropriated $6,000 to build the Big Sable Point Light in Michigan, but the war intervened. By the time Congress reappro-

Built in 1874, the 113-foot-tall Grosse Point Light in Evanston, Illinois, is indicative of the soaring towers built on the lakes between 1870 and 1900. The lantern room of the Grosse Point Light still houses the original second-order Fresnel lens.

The porthole-studded North Point Light in Milwaukee, Wisconsin, stood just thirty feet tall when established in 1855. The brick tower was moved inland and covered in cast-iron plating in 1888. The Bureau of Lighthouses later added an upper steel section to raise the focal plane of the lighthouse to seventy-four feet.

Winslow Lewis and the Lighthouse Establishment built the original Stony Point Light on Lake Ontario in 1830. After the Civil War, the Lighthouse Board replaced the lighthouse with the existing schoolhouse-style light.

priated funds in 1865, the price tag had soared to $35,000, probably due to the rise in cost of construction materials and labor due to the war. The Big Sable Point Light was finally lit for the first time on November 1, 1867.

During the war, many Great Lakes lighthouse keepers, engineers, and inspectors were reassigned to posts within the Union army. The lucky ones returned to lighthouse duty after the war. Some returned with injuries. Keeper James S. Donahue of the South Haven Light (later called the South Haven South Pier Light) in Michigan was wounded twice during the war, the second time resulted in the amputation of one of his legs at the thigh. However, Keeper Donahue wasn't hampered by his war injury; he ably performed his duties as keeper. In fact, the Lighthouse Board credits him with saving fifteen lives during his years of lighthouse ser-

vice, including those of his own two sons. The Board awarded him the Silver Life Saving Medal for his heroic deeds.

One of the odder Civil War legends related to a Great Lakes lighthouse involves the massive second-order Fresnel lens of the Grosse Point Light in Evanston, Illinois. The lens was one of three that the Lighthouse Board purchased in 1860 at a cost of $10,000 apiece. Two of the lenses, including the one that would eventually find its way to Grosse Point, were shipped to Florida for use in lighthouses then under construction. When war broke out, construction stopped. In an effort to protect the valuable lenses, some of the construction workers buried them in an out-of-the-way locale. Apparently, the workers didn't tell the government of their actions, as Secretary of the Treasury Salmon P. Chase issued a report stating that at least one of the lenses had been stolen. When the war ended in 1865, however, the workers returned to the burial spot, dug up the lenses, and sent them back to the Lighthouse Board in Washington. In 1874, one of the lenses lit up the brand-new Grosse Point Light. The lens remains in the tower today.

Another curious fact involves Milwaukee's North Point Light, built in 1855. As with most Great Lakes lighthouses, an engineer working for the Lighthouse Board designed the station. But the North Point engineer was none other than Jefferson Davis, who would later assume the presidency of the Confederacy.

The end of the war prompted a flurry of lighthouse building and rebuilding on the Great Lakes. Between 1865 and 1870, more than three dozen Great Lakes lighthouses were constructed or rebuilt, including the construction of Michigan's Peninsula Point Light in 1866 and Wisconsin's Chequamegon Point Light in 1868. New York's Stony Point Light was rebuilt in 1869.

Around this time, the Lighthouse Board also established central lighthouse supply depots for each of the lighthouse districts. The first of these depots opened at Staten Island, New York, in 1864. In 1869, the first Great Lakes depot opened in Detroit at a temporary location—a building owned by the United States Marine Hospital. In 1874, construction crews finished work on a permanent warehouse on Mount Elliott Avenue near the river, a building which still stands. The depots stocked just about everything needed for lighthouse maintenance—fuel, Fresnel lenses, wicks, paint, buoys, and much more. Tender ships, which brought needed materials (and sometimes inspectors) to lighthouses, were stationed at the district supply depots.

In 1886, the Lighthouse Board increased the number of lighthouse districts in the country to sixteen, with three (up from two) on the Great Lakes. The Ninth District covered all of Lake Michigan, the Tenth encompassed Lakes Erie and Ontario, and the Eleventh covered Lakes Superior, Huron, and St. Clair as well as the rivers connecting them.

Lighthouse Style

Under the watchful eye of the Lighthouse Board, lighthouse construction became standardized in order to save money. After completing a lighthouse, the board reused the plans to build another lighthouse, making modifications in the height and positioning of the tower. A few oddball lights were built, such as Michigan's St. Martin Island Light (1905) with an exoskeleton supporting the

Above, top: *The original third-order Fresnel lens remains in the sky-high lantern room of the Presque Isle Light.*

Above, bottom: *At 113 feet, the "new" Presque Isle Light, established in 1871, is ninety-three feet taller than the Old Presque Isle Light which it replaced.*

The Old Mission Point Light stands eighteen miles due north of Traverse City, Michigan. The lighthouse is a variation on the schoolhouse style.

Built in 1910, Split Rock Light, has an unusual layout: the octagonal tower is attached to a small workroom. Three large keeper's houses stand nearby, where the head keeper, first assistant keeper, second assistant keeper, and their families lived when the station was in operation.

perfectly vertical six-sided tower, but most Great Lakes lights built after 1850 fit loosely into a handful of design categories.

The vast majority of lighthouses built on the Great Lakes before 1867 consisted of a keeper's house, usually built from brick, stone, or wood, with an attached tower or with a tower jutting up from the roof of the dwelling. Lighthouses such as Wisconsin's Potawatomi Light (1838), Ohio's Turtle Island Light (1832), and New York's Selkirk (Salmon River) Light (1838) are all indicative of this design. After 1867, a trend toward considerably taller lighthouses emerged with the brick or iron towers sometimes climbing more than one hundred feet in height. Unlike earlier lighthouses, many of

these taller towers were attached by a passageway to the keeper's house or stood wholly separate from the dwelling. The 113-foot-tall Presque Isle Light (1870) in Michigan and the 108-foot-tall Wind Point Light (1880) in Wisconsin are prime examples of the later, soaring towers.

Several common styles of Great Lakes lighthouses also developed around the middle of the nineteenth century. The schoolhouse style lighthouse, such as Michigan's Old Mission Point Light (1870), features a square tower that rises from the lake side of the dwelling. The Rock Island Light in the St. Lawrence River near Fishers Landing, New York, built in 1847 and rebuilt in 1882, is a prime example of the conical tower

The 108-foot-tall Wind Point Light tower near Racine, Wisconsin, is very similar in design to the towers at Michigan's Presque Isle Light on Lake Huron and Illinois's Grosse Point Light on Lake Michigan. All three lighthouses were designed by Orlando M. Poe of the Army Corps of Engineers. The design, which is repeated at many other lighthouses across the lakes, became known as the Poe style.

design. The pyramidal style had two variations: attached to a keeper's house as was common in Canada, or separate from the house, often on a pierhead, as was popular on Lake Michigan at stations such as the Frankfort North Breakwater Light (1873) in Michigan. Other styles included the cylindrical tower, such as the St. James Harbor (Beaver Island Harbor) Light (1852; rebuilt 1858) in Michigan; the skeletal steel tower, including Wisconsin's Plum Island Rear Range Light (1897); and the tower integrated into a keeper's house on a breakwater, such as the Oswego West Pierhead Light (1822; rebuilt 1934) in New York. A smattering of other styles are seen on the lakes, including the separate octagonal tower notable in Minnesota's Split Rock Light (1910), and the art deco style, typically built on breakwaters after 1930 and never manned. Wisconsin's Port Washington Breakwater Light (1889; rebuilt 1935) is a first-class example of the latter.

Offshore Lights

After 1850, the government funded the construction of offshore lights on the Great Lakes. The first of these lights was built in 1851 on Lake Michigan at Waugoshance Shoal to replace an earlier lightship. To build such lighthouses, construction crews had to build an underwater crib. The crib facilitated construction and helped protect the light station from shifting masses of ice during brutal Great Lakes winters.

The Lighthouse Board built the most famous of these offshore lights at Spectacle Reef, eleven miles east of the Straits of Mackinac in northern Lake Huron. When looking down at the reef, the two rock outcroppings that make up the shoal resemble a giant pair of eyeglasses, a likeness that led to its colorful name. With its proximity to the straits, Spectacle Reef was a major, toothy hazard as little as seven feet below the surface, capable of slicing through the hull of any ship that strayed too near. In the fall of 1867, two vessels sank after bottoming out on the reef. The next year, the Lighthouse Board allocated funds to build a lighthouse on the site.

The initial construction began onshore at Scammon's Harbor in the Les Cheneaux Islands, sixteen miles north of the reef. Workers at Scammon's Harbor constructed a crib to protect the structure. In Detroit, workers assembled a watertight cofferdam; it was then towed to Scammon's Harbor. Construction on the crib and cofferdam began in 1870.

The construction of the circular crib was quite an involved process. A tug towed a flat platform sixteen miles out to the reef where it was moored above the building site in eleven feet of water. Divers examined the reef, marked the platform to conform with variations in the surface of the rock, and then towed the whole structure back to Scammon's Harbor. Workers bolted wedges of timber to the underside of the platform to match the exact topography of the reef. Using ballast stone the crew sank the platform into ten feet of water, moved the crib of round timbers on top of it, and then bolted the crib into place. The diameter of the mammoth crib was ninety-two feet, with an area just shy of a quarter acre. Finally, in the summer of 1871, a boat towed the crib out to Spectacle Reef where it was sunk into position with 1,800 tons of ballast stone.

Meanwhile, the cofferdam arrived in Scammon's Harbor from Detroit. The cofferdam consisted of hundreds of vertical wooden staves, each about fifteen feet long, four inches wide, and six inches thick. They were braced together internally and then hooped and squeezed together with iron belts that wound around the outside of the circular structure. A boat towed the structure out to the reef, where workers sank the cofferdam inside the crib and drove down the individual staves onto the reef to conform to the contours of the rock as closely as possible. Divers used cement to fill any uneven spots, cracks, or holes.

In October 1871, workers began pumping water out of the cofferdam. Once most of the water was out, workers could go inside, stand on the reef eleven feet beneath the surface of Lake Huron, and begin to level out the site. Water continued to trickle in through seams and cracks, but powerful water pumps easily handled the leakage.

Workers built their quarters on the crib where they stayed until winter set in. At the end of October, the crew activated a temporary light and fog signal atop their quarters and halted construction for the season.

A long Great Lakes winter followed. When the construction crew returned to Spectacle Reef on May 20, 1872, a crystal palace of ice towers, chunks, and slabs several feet thick coated the structure. Workers spent several days chopping through the ice to reach the crib and the cofferdam. Though minor repairs were necessary, the structure had withstood its first winter.

Work on the lighthouse continued throughout the summer, including the construction of the limestone tower's base. But Mother Nature was by no means through with the engineers and workmen. In September, a gale blew into northern Lake Huron, a powerful

It took four years to build the ninety-five-foot-tall Spectacle Reef Light in northern Lake Huron east of the Straits of Mackinac. The offshore lighthouse is built on top of a submerged limestone reef that is shaped like a pair of spectacles. (Photo Courtesy of the Great Lakes Historical Society, Vermilion, Ohio)

blast that badly damaged part of the crib and left the workers' quarters in shambles. Workers repaired the damage before construction ended for the season, but over the winter shifting ice completely destroyed the workers' quarters and the temporary beacon on top of it.

Despite all of these hardships, the tower was finally completed in the summer of 1873. When workers returned to prepare the station for activation in May 1874, the light station was once again encased. The pressure of the ice had crushed the tower's entrance door and the ice had forced its way into the interior of the station. Workers again chipped away the ice, aided by increasing late-spring sunshine, and on June 1, 1874, the Spectacle Reef Light brightened the night sky for the first time.

After activation, ice buildup continued to plague the station. Fresh water freezes much harder than salt water, an obstacle of nature that would bedevil America's finest lighthouse engineers at Spectacle Reef and at other

far northern light stations including Stannard Rock Light (1882) off the Upper Peninsula in Lake Superior and Rock of Ages Light (1908) to the north of Stannard Rock near Isle Royale.

Nearly every spring when the keepers returned to the Spectacle Reef Light, they had to chip away great masses of ice. Over time, the crib started to deteriorate from the yearly onslaught. Eventually, workers built an iron caisson around the crib to give further protection. In 1904, workers poured a massive cone of concrete, twenty feet thick at the base and six feet thick at the top, around the tower. In 1921, the crib was surrounded by interlocking steel plates anchored in place by carving a trench around the perimeter of the tower. The beveled tops of the piling helped deflect the encroaching ice in the winters to come. The original Spectacle Reef Light still stands, automated and active after more than 125 Lake Huron winters.

CHAPTER 2

Lighthouse Sweet Lighthouse:

Life in the Great Lakes Lights

Left: *The spectacular, octagonal Kincardine Rear Range Light along the Penetagore River in Kincardine, Ontario, was established in 1881 and was home to a number of keepers for nearly a century until automation in 1978.*

Above: *The red-trimmed windows give the 1869 Sturgeon Point Light on Lake Huron near Harrisville, Michigan, a crisp, clean look.*

For 165 years, Great Lakes lighthouses had keepers. It wasn't easy to become a keeper, as positions were rare and the application process was confusing and biased, to say the least. Once a person became a keeper, the work was difficult and dangerous, and offered little in the way of compensation.

The duties and rules of lighthouse keeping, particularly after 1852, seemed endless. In many ways, the keeper's family worked also, assisting the keeper in all manner of lighthouse chores. Daily life was infinitely more complicated at their remote homes. Food and supplies, medical care, even neighbors were a lengthy, hazardous journey from the lighthouse. Despite the hardship, men and women came forward to serve, attracted for all kinds of reasons to this most peculiar of professions.

I Wanna Be a Great Lakes Lightkeeper

It never was possible to simply sign up to be a Great Lakes lightkeeper. The jobs were scarce, and positions that did open up were fiercely sought after. Before 1896, lighthouse keeper positions were deeply entwined in the American political system. If you wanted to serve at a Great Lakes light station, you pretty much had to know somebody with the influence to make that happen. After 1896, you had to be smart enough to pass the civil service exam and then lucky enough to be selected from a pool of candidates to become a keeper. After the Coast Guard took over operation of American lighthouses in 1939, your chances of becoming a Great Lakes keeper were even more remote due to the various needs of the Coast Guard. You might find yourself in the Caribbean rather than wiling away your time at a Great Lakes lighthouse. Today, of course, the job no longer exists. But, from the establishment of American lighthouses on the Great Lakes in 1819 until relatively recently, someone had to maintain Great Lakes lighthouses, and there was indeed a "system" in place from the beginning that matched keepers with stations and kept the lights burning when mariners needed them.

Almost all of the early Great Lakes lightkeepers owed their jobs to political connections, political debts, and general political corruption. The local collector of customs, himself a political appointee, was responsible for the nomination of the lighthouse keepers in his district; the Secretary of the Treasury would then make the official appointment. The vast majority of the time, the Secretary simply appointed the recommended candidate, giving considerable power to the local collectors of customs. This system, in place until 1896, nearly guaranteed the appointment of keepers on the basis of evening out political debts or for other murky reasons.

Of course, this doesn't mean that keepers who got in based on their political connections were incompetent—some of the most celebrated of Great Lakes keepers were hired through this system. Others were quietly competent and worked for years at their light stations without incident. But there were plenty of examples of politically connected yet bumbling keepers who were hardly qualified to do just about any job, much less keep a lighthouse.

Colonel George McDougall Jr. was such a keeper. Before accepting the appointment as the first keeper of Michigan's Fort Gratiot Light, he worked as an attorney. He wasn't a particularly effective lawyer, as Michigan courts had barred McDougall from practicing law several times during his career. McDougall was known to drink heavily both in his spare time and on the job. He was also rather meanspirited, possibly due to the copious amounts of liquor in his system.

Despite his background, McDougall was able to secure a posting as a lighthouse keeper because he knew the right people. Detroit's Collector of Customs William Woodbridge was a friend of McDougall's. McDougall did a little arm-twisting, and maybe even plied Woodbridge with a wee bit of spirits. Woodbridge agreed to recommend McDougall for the position of keeper of the new Fort Gratiot Light. In 1825, McDougall assumed his post.

Not long after his appointment, McDougall found his duties at the station to be a bit of a nuisance. So he hired an assistant to do the actual work at the lighthouse—while he retained the title of keeper. Having an assistant at the helm was probably a good thing for the mariners who relied on the Fort Gratiot Light, as Keeper McDougall continued to sip spirits while "on duty." Of course, the assistant's help cost money, so McDougall persuaded Woodbridge to appoint him deputy director of customs as well, adding $150 to his $350 annual lightkeeper's salary. Later in his career, McDougall also served as postmaster of the town of Port Huron, a job he got through friend and Secretary of War Lewis Cass. McDougall held all three appointments until his death in 1842.

If an aspiring lightkeeper didn't have political connections, there were several other qualities that helped secure an appointment as a Great Lakes lighthouse keeper. Military service was generally a prerequisite. This

Colonel George McDougall Jr. was the first keeper of Michigan's Fort Gratiot Light. He assumed his post in 1825.

The overriding duty of all Great Lakes lightkeepers was to keep the Fresnel lenses—like this one from Point Aux Barques, on display at the Point Aux Barques Life-Saving Station— burning brightly from sunset to sunrise.

The lantern room of the Sand Hills Light on Lake Superior was where the keeper on watch would climb to observe the weather or to look for vessels in distress.

was particularly true after the Civil War when anyone who hadn't fought for the Union army was immediately suspect.

Keepers often were former sailors, men with hearts married to the lakes, who now wanted to settle down to safer work ashore. Before 1852, when an age limit for newly hired keepers was set, many old sailors retired from their lives on the water to live out the remainder of their days as lighthouse keepers.

But actual standards for lighthouse keepers were vague, at best. In 1852, the newly formed Lighthouse Board set some basic qualifications, including the ability to read and write, an understanding of rudimentary mathematics, a talent for boatmanship, and the capability to write and file accurate reports with the Lighthouse Board. The board also set an age range between eighteen and fifty for new hires, though once a keeper

was in the service, there was no mandatory retirement age. The Lighthouse Board also set standards that would allow for the dismissal of a keeper including failure of keeping the light lit, leaving the station without official permission, and drinking on the job.

Of course, setting such fundamental requirements didn't address the problem of political appointees. The Lighthouse Board continued to nominate keepers based on the recommendations of the local collector of customs. By the 1870s, however, the Board began to interview the recommended keeper candidates before appointing them.

Further changes were brewing. The Pendleton Civil Service Act of 1883 required all federal employees to pass exams, though President Chester A. Arthur had the authority to exempt certain categories of federal employees. Arthur exempted lightkeepers, and it wasn't until President Grover Cleveland issued an executive order on May 6, 1896, that lighthouse keeper appointments finally came under the Pendleton Act. After 1896, lists of eligible candidates who had passed the exams were drawn up by local civil service boards, and district engineers chose the lighthouse keepers. The days of political favoritism in the lighthouse service had finally come to an end.

Keepers' Duties

According to the Lighthouse Board's *Instructions to Light-Keepers*, the overriding duty of all Great Lakes lighthouse keepers was that the "lights must be lighted punctually at sunset, and must be kept burning at full intensity until sunrise." Everything a keeper did at a light station revolved around this basic responsibility, and

failure to meet this requisite was grounds for immediate dismissal. After all, the purpose of a lighthouse is to mark the shoreline or hazards during nighttime.

The watchroom below the lantern room was the center of operations for a light station; almost all Great Lakes lighthouses have a watchroom. When lightkeepers used oil to light their beacons, they stored pressure tanks filled with fuel in the watchroom. During the night a keeper was always on duty in this room, monitoring the light, watching the fuel level, maintaining the turning mechanism, climbing into the lantern room to observe the weather and to look out over the lake or river for signs of distressed vessels, and activating the fog signal when needed. At lighthouses with more than one keeper, which was quite common at Great Lakes lighthouses, the keepers worked in shifts during the night,

Assistant Keeper Tom Hassing cleans the third-order bivalve lens at Minnesota's Split Rock Light in 1946. (Photo by Minneapolis Star Tribune, *Minnesota Historical Society)*

After 1888, the Lighthouse Board required keepers to paint light stations themselves, including the painting of the tower's exterior. This was a daunting task at stations such as Seul Choix Point in Upper Michigan, which had an eighty-foot tower.

From its establishment in 1895 until the day this automated modern optic was installed at Seul Choix Point Light in 1972, at least one keeper was always on duty while the light was lit.

though all keepers remained on duty when the weather turned bad. Many Great Lakes light stations only had one keeper, and that keeper maintained the beacon throughout the night alone, regardless of conditions.

During the Great Lakes shipping season, the keepers had to complete, by 10 A.M. daily, all preparations for relighting the lighthouse. They had to clean the lens and the lantern windows, polish the reflectors, clean and fill the lamp, test the flashing mechanism, dust the whole apparatus, and trim the wicks in the lamp. Trimming the wicks was standard before lighthouses were electrified in the twentieth century. This daily chore led to the widespread nickname "wickies" for lighthouse keepers.

Keepers spent the rest of the day polishing brass parts, organizing supplies in the watchroom, and sweeping the stairs and landings. To make sweeping easier, the government standardized the design of the spiral stairways, using a cast-iron staircase with grated steps made up of football-shaped holes. The holes allowed the debris to fall all the way to the bottom of the tower, where it could be easily swept into a dustpan. This design was particularly useful in the colder months at Great Lakes stations, when a keeper tracked snow and ice onto the stairs. The snow and ice would melt and drip off the stairs. Such staircases are still in place in numerous Great Lakes light towers, including Michigan's Big Sable Point Light and New York's Charlotte-Genesee Light.

Many other duties at a typical Great Lakes light station were not directly related to maintaining a lighted beacon during the night. After 1888, lighthouse keepers were required to paint the station, inside and out, and

Over the years, many keepers passed through this door to climb the tower stairs of the Seul Choix Point Light.

to tackle minor maintenance problems. When Peter Coughlin became keeper of Wisconsin's Eagle Bluff Light on February 5, 1919, he spent the first few months painting everything at the station, included the interior and exterior of the keeper's house, the tower, the oil house, the outhouse, and the fence around the keeper's house. To paint the tower, he used a homemade scaffolding common throughout the Bureau of Lighthouses, in which a chair or barrel is suspended from the balcony with ropes. Although it was standard for keepers such as Coughlin to paint the station after a transfer from another station, many Great Lakes keepers arrived at their posts every year well before the shipping season opened to allow themselves enough time to paint the entire station. After all, chipped or faded paint inside or out would not sit well with the district inspector.

The Lighthouse Service required keepers to maintain a log of their supplies used and to submit the tally to the district at the end of the shipping season. This

Above: *The Seul Choix Point Light has been restored, and the interior of the station looks much as it did for the first keeper in 1895. Each day, keepers and their families often had to cook for a number of people. At stag stations, the keeper stuck with the last watch of the night had to make breakfast.*

Right: *Keepers often wore more-casual clothes for daily duties at the light station, but they always kept a uniform pressed and ready to be quickly slipped on when the inspector's tender ship approached.*

way the government would know exactly how much fuel, paint, soap, food, toilet paper, and all other provisions the lightkeepers and their families used annually. The government used these totals to allocate supplies the following season.

The Station Watchbook

After about 1820, the Lighthouse Establishment required keepers to maintain a daily log in a watchbook of happenings at the station. The keepers recorded the precise times they lit and extinguished the beacon, the weather, the number and types of ships that passed, and noteworthy events such as shipwrecks, visits by inspectors, keeper absences from the station, etc. However, the keepers had to be brief, as only two one-sided pages were allocated for each *month*. Personal comments were to be kept to a minimum.

Keepers' adherence to the brevity rule varied. Keeper Martin Knudsen of Wisconsin's Pilot Island Light used the log to record the birds he saw during the winter of 1895–96, including "titmice, thrushes, and a hawk." An 1875 entry in the log by Keeper James Corgan of Lake Superior's Manitou Island Light read: "July 15. Principal Keeper started at 8:00 P.M. in the station boat with wife for Copper Harbor (distant 14 miles), in anticipation of an increase soon after arriving. When one and one half miles east of Horseshoe Harbor, Mrs. Corgan gave birth to a rollicking boy; all things lovely, had everything comfortable aboard. Sea a dead calm."

The watchbooks often offer the only direct record of daily life at the station, and even in their brevity, the emotional impact of events is starkly illustrated. After Eagle Bluff Keeper Peter Coughlin's wife Margaret died suddenly on April 1, 1925, the keeper's entries, usually made in firm strokes, were so shaky they were hard to recognize. Keeper Coughlin would retire the following year. In the log of White River lightkeeper William Robinson on July 30, 1874, he had written simply: "Died at the light station, my infant son aged 26 days."

Inspections

When the Lighthouse Board took over the administration of lighthouses in 1852, it instituted surprise inspections of all stations at least once a year. The district inspector would arrive on the tender ships, which traveled to stations regularly bringing supplies. To allow keepers enough time to get everything in order, inspectors flew a special flag from the mast of the tender to show they were aboard and sounded the ship's horn as

Above, top: *The head keeper at Seul Choix Point Light kept his bedroom neat. There was no time for extensive tidying between the first warning of an inspector's approach and his arrival.*

Above, bottom: *The dressing table in the master bedroom of Seul Choix Point Light. Inspectors were known to check under beds and in drawers to make sure everything was shipshape.*

Above: *The Sturgeon Point Light remains active, but the white-washed exterior and the lipstick-red trim reflect the efforts of the Alcona Historical Society, which restored the station.*

Right: *Keepers served at Michigan's Sturgeon Point Light on Lake Huron from its establishment in 1869 until the light was automated in 1939.*

they approached a station. Keepers, particularly after the advent of radio and telephone communications, also routinely warned fellow keepers of inspectors in the area.

It is said the first thing the inspector would examine was the brass dustpan, standard issue at Great Lakes lighthouses. A polished dustpan was the mark of a well-run station. Of course, keepers often controlled what the inspector saw to enhance their image. The keepers at Michigan's South Fox Island station kept a tool board full of cleaned and polished tools, which they never used for repair work. They stowed a toolbox containing the set of tools they actually used away from the prying eyes of the inspector.

The inspectors, of course, examined the lantern room with its precious lens to make sure everything was clean and operating properly. They also checked the supplies of critical things such as fuel and wicks, as well as the records of supplies used, to make sure the numbers added up. Inspectors checked the interior woodwork and floors to ensure everything was freshly painted. They also examined most other aspects of life at a lighthouse, going so far as to look in dresser drawers to make sure clothing was neatly folded and opening the oven door to check that no dirty dishes had been hidden inside. After 1884, the Lighthouse Board issued uniforms, and all male lighthouse keepers were required to be in uniform when the inspector arrived. Female lightkeepers, who were not issued uniforms, were expected to be neatly dressed. Children were to be clean, well-mannered, and kept out of the way of the inspector. For all but the most rambunctious children, this wasn't a problem, as most kids sensed something was up and looked at the inspectors with a sense of awe. Joseph St. Andre, who lived as a child at the Marquette Harbor Light and the Keweenaw Waterway Lower Entry Light, both in Michigan, described the arrival of the inspector as the "second coming of the Lord."

After the Bureau of Lighthouses took over operations of lighthouses in 1910, inspectors began to award keepers for efficiency by issuing Efficiency Stars—which could be worn on a keeper's uniform after several consecutive positive inspections—and the Efficiency Pennant—which was flown from the station for one year after it was awarded to the most efficient lighthouse in every district.

Keepers as Tour Guides

Today, it is a given that a lighthouse will attract tourists. But the tradition of visiting lighthouses actually dates back more than a century. The Lighthouse Board recog-

nized early on that public relations would play a role in a keeper's life. The fourth article in the first chapter of *Instructions to Light-Keepers* states that "keepers must be courteous and polite to all visitors and show them everything of interest about the station at such times as will not interfere with light-house duties." Though stations had restrictions about where visitors could go to avoid dirtying or damaging equipment, many keepers made their stations remarkably accessible to the curious.

Some keepers seemed to thrive in the public eye. Keeper Charles "Cap" Hunter, who served at Ohio's Marblehead Light from 1903 to 1933, certainly loved the tourists who ventured out to the lighthouse from nearby Sandusky. A storyteller by nature, Cap reveled in a well-spun tale—some completely true, some rather embellished. Embellishment was often not needed, however. The ferocious storms that regularly struck Lake Erie and the ships and lives lost in the lake's swirling waters gave the keeper plenty of fodder for spinning his yarns.

Franklin D. Covell, head keeper of Minnesota's Split Rock Light from 1928 to 1944, found himself with little time to entertain visitors. When the North Shore Highway opened along Lake Superior in 1924, the once-remote lighthouse high on a cliff far from any city, was suddenly accessible to the masses of tourists traveling the new highway that passed very near the light station. Within seven years, 5,000 visitors a year, almost all during the summer months, visited the station. By 1938, Keeper Covell estimated 100,000 people stopped by. As a keeper was required to escort all visitors, such numbers posed a major problem to the efficient operation of the station. So Keeper Covell established visiting hours to keep tourists away from Split Rock at critical times. He also closed the lantern room to visitors after he found scratches on the station's third-order bivalve Fresnel lens. By 1936, the Bureau of Lighthouses recognized the heavy-visitation problem at Split Rock and assigned an extra keeper during the summer just to handle the tourists.

Salary and Fringe Benefits

Becoming a lighthouse keeper wasn't exactly the road to riches. The first Great Lakes lightkeepers earned an average of $250 a year, a paltry sum even back in 1819. Even with so much room for growth, the rise in keeper salaries was hardly meteoric. By the 1840s, Great Lakes keepers were earning only around $400 per year. After the Lighthouse Board took over in 1852, salaries were

After a long day of polishing and cleaning the lens and the station and before they had to stand watch throughout the night, keepers often relaxed in the sitting room, such as this one at Sturgeon Point Light.

The keepers at Minnesota's Split Rock Light pose for the camera in summer shirtsleeves, circa 1945. (Photo courtesy of Minnesota Historical Society)

William Robinson, the first keeper at the White River Light on the western coast of Michigan, served at the quaint station for forty-seven years. On the day he was to retire, Keeper Robinson died at the lighthouse.

The last keepers left the Charlotte-Genessee Light in Rochester, New York, in 1881. That year, the nearby Rochester Harbor Light replaced the 1822 light station.

for the first time broken down by position at a lighthouse. Head keepers on Great Lakes lights earned up to $600, and assistants made about half that. Keepers at offshore lights and at lighthouses that required extra duties—such as maintaining more than one light, tending a buoy, etc.—received bonus pay on top of the standard salaries.

Even after being adjusted for inflation, all of these salaries would translate to well below $10,000 annually in 2002 dollars. And these numbers were averages; as late as 1896, Henry H. Gattie became keeper of the Baileys Harbor Range Lights in Wisconsin at a salary of only $540 year—incidentally, the same salary received by Baileys Harbor Keeper Joseph Harris Jr. in 1875, twenty-one years earlier.

Pay finally nudged upward by the 1920s, with head keepers at large stations with fog signals earning a base salary of as much as $1,740 annually. The government paid further incentives for duty at particularly remote stations such as Stannard Rock and Menagerie Island (Isle Royale).

Of course, keepers did have certain fringe benefits. Most of the Great Lakes light stations had a keeper's house, where the keeper and his family could live for free. The government supplied most food staples, which saved the keeper and his family a considerable amount of money. Today, it is easy to envy a keeper's lack of commuting expenses.

However, some basic benefits available to other federal employees were not made available to lighthouse keepers until the twentieth century, including health benefits, a pension plan, and disability benefits. Though the personnel of lightships had access to free medical care from the U.S. Public Health Service, lightkeepers did not receive the same benefit until 1916. A pension plan was finally extended to lighthouse keepers in 1918, and keepers disabled on the job were covered by 1925.

So, those drawn to serve at lighthouses had to strike a certain balance: The meager pay was offset somewhat by the fringe benefits, but for those enamored with the open water, the thing that tipped the scales in favor of service was a chance to be near their mistress, the Lakes. Then again, for many a Great Lakes keeper, tending the light wasn't the only way to make a buck.

Moonlighting

Great Lakes keepers got involved in a wide variety of activities to bring in extra income, ranging from noble positions in public service to serious skullduggery and intrigue. Most keepers engaged in practical professions somewhere between the two extremes.

If the outside work did not interfere with a keeper's duties, the government did not forbid keepers from moonlighting. Great Lakes keepers found extra work as fishermen, boat builders, harbor pilots, farmers, coopers, and carpenters.

Keeper Burt Hill, who served at the Sand Island Light in the Apostle Islands until 1941, worked on the side as a postmaster and also ran a co-op store. His wife, Anna Mae, supplemented the family income by cooking meals for fishermen and tourists. Keeper Godtfried M. S. Hansen of Door County's Pilot Island Light moonlighted as a notary public, and one keeper at Lake Superior's Rock of Ages Light off Isle Royale was a sought-after taxidermist.

William Duclon, keeper of Wisconsin's Eagle Bluff Light, from 1883 to 1918, earned extra money ice fishing with his sons during the off-season. In the spring of 1887, the Duclons pulled 2,000 pounds of lake trout through the ice, selling their catch in town for a tidy sum.

Some Great Lakes keepers also worked as justices of the peace and even as preachers, but others had their eye on more nefarious sources of income. Keeper Nathaniel Fadden of the Manitou Island Light on Lake Superior built himself a still at the light station and made liquor to sell to the local Native Americans. His operation was later discovered by the Lighthouse Board, and Keeper Fadden was removed from his post and jailed.

Food and Water

Great Lakes lighthouse keepers looked forward to the quarterly arrival of tender ships which carried their supply of food staples courtesy of the federal government. The Lighthouse Board supplied each keeper and each member of their families with an annual total of 200 pounds of pork, 100 pounds of beef, 2 barrels of flour, 50 pounds of rice, 50 pounds of brown sugar, 24 pounds of coffee, 10 gallons of beans or peas, 4 gallons of vinegar, and 2 barrels of potatoes. Salt was also provided.

Despite what seems on the surface to be a substantial amount of table fare, most Great Lakes keepers and their families augmented their food supplies by growing gardens, hunting, fishing, berry picking, raising livestock, and, for those close to towns, grocery shopping. During World War I, securing outside food sources was promoted heavily by the Bureau of Lighthouses to ease the shortage of food for troops abroad.

Above: *Many Great Lakes lighthouses, including the Michigan Island Old (First) Light and the Michigan Island (Second) Light in the Apostle Islands in Lake Superior, stood in wilderness areas far from civilization. Self-reliance was essential for lighthouse families, as assistance could be days away.*

Right: *The keeper of the Baileys Harbor Range Lights and his family did not have to go far to find neighbors with whom to socialize. Keeper Joseph Harris Jr., who served here from 1875 until 1881, loved to chew the fat over a glass of lemonade with anyone who made the short walk from the village of Baileys Harbor to the Rear Range Light and keeper's house.*

The Whitefish Point Light and the Copper Harbor Light were the first lighthouses built on Lake Superior. Born in Sweden, keeper Robert Carlson served at Whitefish Point Light from 1903 until 1931. In 1914, Keeper Carlson rescued eleven men from the capsized fishing tug Ora Endress. *In 1975, the* Edmund Fitzgerald *sank off this same point.*

Gardens sprouted at stations from Lake Superior's North Shore to the foot of Lake Ontario. Keepers grew lettuce, rhubarb, radishes, carrots, beans, corn, peas, potatoes, and much more, depending on the soil and climatic conditions at their station. With the exceptions of offshore reef lights and a few of the lights on rocky isles with no plant life, nearly every Great Lakes lighthouse had at least a small garden. Even some of the lighthouses on rocky isles had gardens grown in dirt hauled out from shore.

Many Great Lakes keepers and their families hunted to further supplement food supplies. Keeper Henry H. Gattie of the Baileys Harbor Range Lights in Wisconsin killed a hearty 175-pound whitetail buck near the station during the 1897 deer season. Keepers at the Menagerie Island (Isle Royale) Light hopped in the station's sailboat and set out for much larger Isle Royale to hunt the resident moose population. Some hunters went after other large game such as black bears and wolves,

while other keepers hunted smaller quarry, including grouse, rabbits, squirrels, and ducks. Keepers often cleaned and dried or salted fresh meat for later consumption, but other stations canned fresh meat. At some Great Lakes stations, storage containers of perishable goods were attached to a tether and lowered into the frigid lake waters. A few keepers even built unofficial icehouses, harvesting ice in the wintertime and storing it in sawdust for use to keep meat cold and drinks cool during the summer.

Given the wide expanse of open water available to just about every lighthouse keeper, fishing was another popular and nearly universal way Great Lakes keepers diversified their diets. Lake trout, walleye, chubs, perch, sturgeon, whitefish, and many other freshwater fish graced keepers' tables throughout the region. Keepers often fished simply to kill time during their off-duty hours, and at some stations, fish were about the only type of meat the keepers ate.

The existing Eagle Harbor Light on Upper Michigan's Lake Superior coast was built for $14,000 in 1871.

heading over to the general store. Of course, any items purchased locally ate up part of a keeper's income, so most "urban" keepers kept trips to the market to a minimum. However, temptations—such as chocolate, canned foods, and fresh bread—lured the keepers, occasionally causing them to stray from their budget.

Lightkeepers obtained water for drinking and washing from a variety of sources. As on many saltwater stations, some Great Lakes lighthouses collected rainwater. Water would run off the roof during rainstorms and into gutters that funneled the water into pipes leading to a cistern, usually housed in the basement. Michigan's White River Light had such a system, as did Minnesota's Split Rock Light. The system was dependent on regular rainfall and was of little use during a drought. Debris from the roof—dirt, bird droppings, leaves—also could be washed into the cistern with the water. Keepers solved this problem by installing vents in the piping or spouts that swung out from the gutters. The keeper would open the vents or swing out the spouts at the first sign of sprinkles to allow the contaminated water to spill onto the ground when the rain started. After a few minutes, the keeper closed the vents or swung in the spouts, redirecting the now-clean water into the cistern. The government also instructed keepers to put a little powdered chalk in the cistern water and stir it up every once in awhile to neutralize the lead in the water. Other than a little diligence at the start of a rainstorm and an occasional dash of chalk, the cistern system required little effort and worked quite well.

Unlike ocean-side lighthouses, the Great Lakes stations were sitting along, or in the middle of, fresh water. Although many people might be hesitant to take a swig of unfiltered Great Lakes water today, keepers and their families worked at a time when the lakes weren't polluted with industrial and agricultural runoff. Keepers and their families didn't hesitate to drink the lake water, and there doesn't seem to be a record anywhere of death or disease coming to keepers who took a slurp from a Great Lake. Stations utilizing lake water, such as Chambers Island Light in the middle of Green Bay, simply carried the water up from the shore in buckets and filled storage containers. A few Great Lakes stations, such as Michigan's Fourteen Mile Point Light, had a more deluxe setup, featuring a windmill that pumped water from the lake into holding tanks. Many other stations had a well. Even some of the stations with the cistern system used a well, with a cistern system in place to provide water for washing and as an emergency reserve.

Many Great Lakes lighthouses featured gutters on the roof that channeled water into pipes that emptied into cisterns in the basement. The water was then pumped into the kitchen for household use.

Before automation took place at stations on the more remote islands and shoals, tender ships carried fresh water out to the stations and pumped it directly into a lighthouse's water storage tanks. At many of these stations it was not possible to drill a well, and by the twentieth century, people were aware of the potential risk in drinking rain water or water straight from the lake.

Keepers at Play

Most Great Lakes keepers, holed up in a light station on a lonely point, isolated island, or remote shoal, found time away from their lighthouse duties to take up a hobby or two to pass the time. Many a keeper spent his or her free time reading, birdwatching, collecting shells and agates, painting, playing games, or writing poems under the warm sun and cool breezes of a Great Lakes summer day, idling away the hours before the evening watch began.

Great Lakes lighthouse keepers and their families engaged in a wide variety of hobbies and pastimes. Keeper William Duclon, who served at Eagle Bluff Light from 1883 to 1918, formed a band with his family. The piano they used is still at the station.

Many Great Lakes keepers played musical instruments. Keeper Franklin J. Covell of Minnesota's Split Rock Light livened up family gatherings at the station with nimble ditties on his fiddle. Keeper William Duclon of the Eagle Bluff Light in Wisconsin rounded up his family members and formed a traveling band, known perhaps a little unoriginally as the Duclon Band. The Duclons were serious about music. The traveling band purchased a rare violin and an old upright piano, hauling the latter between gigs on a sleigh or wagon, depending on the snowpack.

Beginning in 1876, the Lighthouse Board circulated portable libraries of forty to fifty books to the stations by tender ship. The libraries traveled within an oak carrying case with doors that folded open to reveal books, including tales of the sea, popular fiction, works of history, and books on scientific topics. The libraries rotated between stations on the Lakes every three months

or so, every book having been easily devoured within that amount of time. The arrival of a new library often set off a frenzy of activity.

Most Great Lakes lighthouses were surrounded by wilderness, and many lightkeepers liked to explore the frontier surroundings. Stories of Great Lakes lightkeepers fascinated by botany, geology, astronomy, and wildlife biology abound. Sometimes the keepers didn't even have to leave the station to come face-to-face with nature. In 1872, a keeper at Lake Superior's Grand Island Old North Light recorded an incident with a nighttime visitor in his watchbook: "At 2:30 A.M. an eared owl (the large kind) sat perched upon the railing of the tower, as sedate and important as a judge advocate upon a court-martial."

Many early visitors to Great Lakes lights recognized the majesty of the wilderness of light stations. In August 1880, Ben Fagg of Sturgeon Bay visited the Pilot Island Light in Lake Michigan. Fagg reveled in his wilderness surroundings, writing "On moonlit nights it is like being in a dream of ideality to walk alone over the moss-covered rocks and listen to the swish of the breakers that break over the breakwater at the boat landing, hear them roaring on all sides of the little island, and to see huge vessels under full sail crossing the moonglade on their way through the Door. One seems to be completely separated from all that is worldly and bad. There is no field gossip out here. The land is not suitable for general farming purposes, but it is a splendid place to raise an ample crop of good, pure thoughts."

Others found a sense of power living in the vast wilderness. Keeper Alexander McLean of the Michigan Island Old (First) Light in Lake Superior's Apostle Islands loved his isolated surroundings and gushed about the remote island "where I was the only human being for whole months, monarch of all I surveyed."

Some keepers stationed at lighthouses near towns preferred a healthy social life over quiet reflection or isolation in the woods. Keeper Joseph Harris Jr. of the Baileys Harbor Range Lights on Lake Michigan was active within the nearby community of Baileys Harbor, founding a debating society and a G.A.R. (Grand Army of the Republic) post with fellow Union veterans. The keeper's house itself was a magnet for townspeople, who liked to stop by for a glass of lemonade and a visit with the Harris family on warm summer days. Keepers at stations in or near cities, such as the Erie Land Light in Erie, Pennsylvania, and the Grosse Point Light in Evanston, Illinois, near Chicago, enjoyed very active

Harriet Colfax served as keeper of the Old Michigan City Light in Michigan City, Indiana, for forty-three years. The legendary keeper died just five months after retiring in 1904.

social lives from their keepers' houses. The communities accepted the lighthouse cottages as any other. Lighthouses were simply lakefront houses that happened to have a tower attached.

Great Lakes Lighthouse Married Life

At most light stations, the keeper's home life was closely connected to the lighthouse. At many Great Lakes lighthouses, the Lighthouse Board considered it a strong advantage for a keeper to be married, particularly if the keeper had children. The larger the family, the more free labor the government could count on at the light station. Companionship was also considered important for the sanity of a keeper, who without a family, may well develop a tendency to sit around and ponder his loneliness, driving himself mad in the process. Family men were also widely considered to be more responsible in their duties.

At some lighthouses, the government *required* a newly hired keeper to be married. When the Menagerie Island (Isle Royale) Light in Lake Superior was com-

pleted in 1875, one of the men who worked on the construction crew, an Irish immigrant named Francis Malone, applied for the position of assistant lighthouse keeper with the district inspector. The district inspector told Malone, a bachelor, that the keepers at the station needed to be married. So Malone went to Houghton on the Michigan mainland, found a willing young lass, and promptly married her. The district inspector subsequently appointed him the assistant keeper, and Malone later became the head keeper of the Menagerie Island Light. Malone and his wife went on to raise twelve kids at the station, all of whom pitched in with the lighthouse duties.

Great Lakes lightkeepers' wives were deeply involved in the operations of the light station, helping keep the light often without pay and sometimes officially as Lighthouse Board–appointed assistant keepers. The Lighthouse Board recognized that hiring and retaining capable assistant keepers was very difficult, and appointing a keeper's wife, if she was willing, brought a sense of stability to the staff at remote stations.

MICHIGAN CITY'S HARRIET COLFAX

To serve forty-three years as a Great Lakes lighthouse keeper is an impressive accomplishment. But to tend *two* Great Lakes lighthouses simultaneously for thirty-three of those years is an amazing feat. Most Great Lakes keepers who had reached such a great number of years of service were men. They started young and had families to help them out. The grueling and dangerous work of tending two lighthouses seemed beyond the capacity of a single person. But in Michigan City, Indiana, keeper Harriet Colfax did all of this, most of the time by herself, and became a legend in the process.

A former voice and piano teacher, Harriet Colfax became a lightkeeper of the Old Michigan City Light in 1861 on the recommendation of her cousin Schuyler Colfax, a congressman who later became vice president under President Ulysses S. Grant.

Once on the job, Harriet Colfax proved herself a capable keeper of the beacon while earning her initial annual salary of $350. She maintained the beacon, cleaned and polished the lamps and lens, painted the interior of the buildings, and logged important information such as the weather, visitors, shipwrecks, and other happenings in her watchbook. She grew a garden, hauled supplies, cut wood, rowed the lighthouse dinghy to attend to things in the harbor, and rescued sailors in distress. Her inspection reports were exemplary. Records indicate that she operated her station with efficiency.

Initially, she was responsible only for the Old Michigan City Light on shore, but in November 1871, when the Lighthouse Board built Michigan City East Pierhead Light at the mouth of Trail Creek in Michigan City, that light also became Keeper Colfax's responsibility.

The Michigan City East Pierhead Light was built on a pier stretching 1,500 feet into Lake Michigan. Although the pier featured an elevated wooden and metal catwalk, the walk to and from the pierhead light could be very hazardous in rough weather. "Went to the beacon tonight with considerable risk of life," Keeper Colfax wrote in her log on September 29, 1872, the night of a strong westerly gale. One blustery evening in 1886, she had just returned to shore after lighting the beacon when above the howl of the wind she heard a splintering crack. She turned just in time to see the pierhead light topple into the lake.

Bad weather only made an already tough task more difficult. The lard oil used in the lamps at the time needed to be heated to a high temperature to burn properly. There was no heat source at the East Pierhead Light, so to light the beacon, Keeper Colfax had to heat lard oil on the potbellied cookstove in the Old Michigan City Light's keeper's house on shore and quickly carry the pan of hot oil out to the pierhead beacon. If the lard oil cooled too much before she could get to the lighthouse, she had to go back to the shore lighthouse, reheat the oil, and then return to the beacon with the hot oil until she could get it lit properly. Keeper Colfax must have been thrilled in 1882 when she received word that the old lard oil lamps would be replaced with lamps fueled by kerosene, a gas that didn't have to be heated in order to be lit.

Harriet Colfax retired on October 12, 1904, at the age of eighty. She died just five months later. The Old Michigan City Light and the Michigan City East Pierhead Light (rebuilt in 1904) still stand. Today, Old Michigan City Light houses a museum operated by the Michigan City Historical Society.

Assistant Keeper Anna Carlson, wife of Keeper Robert Carlson of Michigan's Whitefish Point Light, kept the light in an official capacity. In addition to her regular duties, she helped in the rescue of eleven men aboard the sinking fishing tug *Ora Endress*, a rescue that led to official commendation—for her husband. Sarah Sanderson, the wife of Keeper William Sanderson of Wisconsin's Cana Island Light, was also appointed assistant keeper after her husband became the initial keeper of the lighthouse when it was activated in 1870. Her annual salary of $400 greatly improved the family's financial position, raising the household's income to a respectable $1,000 per year. The good times wouldn't last, however. In 1882, Congress did not pass appropriations to pay her salary or the salaries of a number of other wives who were assistant keepers. Sarah Sanderson's position was officially eliminated. She continued her work without pay until her husband left Cana Island in 1891.

There was also an unofficial rule under the Lighthouse Board that a keeper's wife would be appointed keeper of a station upon the death of her husband. These appointments were often motivated by compassion, as keepers' families received no death benefits, and a lighthouse family would often be left with no means of support after the death of the keeper. Appointing a keeper's wife, or, more rarely, his daughter, was simply the right thing to do. Most Great Lakes female keepers gained their positions in this way.

The first female keeper on the Great Lakes was Rachel Wolcott, who took over as keeper of Ohio's Marblehead Light after the death of her husband Benajah in 1832. Her appointment was short-lived, however, as she married Jeremiah Van Beschoten two years later, and Van Beschoten was subsequently appointed keeper of Marblehead Light.

However, some female keepers continued in their work for many years after their husband's death. Elizabeth Whitney Van Riper Williams was married to Clement Van Riper when he was appointed keeper of the St. James Harbor (Beaver Island Harbor) Light on Lake Michigan in 1869. Keeper Van Riper drowned in 1872 during an attempt to rescue sailors from a sinking schooner in the harbor; his body was never found. Upon his death, Elizabeth took over as keeper. Although she would remarry, she never got over the tragic loss of her first husband. In her 1905 autobiography *A Child of the Sea; and Life Among the Mormons*, she wrote: "Only those who have passed through the same know what a sorrow it is to lose your loved one by drowning and not be able to recover the remains. It is a sorrow that never ends through life." However, she found meaning in her work, adding, with a touch of turn-of-the-century melodrama: "Though the life that was dearest to me had gone . . . there were others out on the dark and treacherous waters who needed to catch the rays of the shining light from my light-house tower." She would serve forty-one years as keeper at St. James Harbor and at the Little Traverse Light on the Michigan mainland, assuaging her grief just a little bit every night when she lit the beacon under her watch.

In 1872, Elizabeth Whitney Van Riper Williams became keeper of the St. James Harbor (Beaver Island Harbor) Light upon the death of her husband, Keeper Clement Van Riper. She later remarried but remained a keeper, subsequently serving at Michigan's Little Traverse Point Light.

Right: *The Lighthouse Board deactivated the Old Presque Isle Light upon the activation of the "new" Presque Isle Light in 1871.*

Facing page: *During the Civil War, President Abraham Lincoln appointed Patrick Garraty keeper of the Old Presque Isle Light.*

Above: *The Point Betsie Light harbored keepers from the time of its establishment in 1858 until automation in 1983. The station was one of the last American lights on the Great Lakes with a keeper.*

Right: *A breakwater of steel plating protects the Point Betsie Light from the surging waters of Lake Michigan.*

Kids and Lighthouses

Many Great Lakes keepers and their wives raised children at light stations. As noted earlier, older children were often expected to help maintain the station. Younger kids enjoyed a unique childhood, punctuated with adventure, endless mischief, and a certain amount of danger.

Educating kids was a difficult issue for keepers' families. The Lighthouse Board made an effort to appoint keepers with school-age children to stations near schools, and some keepers with kids swapped positions with non-parenting keepers nearer to town, but not everyone could make such arrangements. Sometimes the keepers had to pay to board their families in town so the children could attend school, not an easy task on a keeper's meager salary. Other children lived at the lighthouse but had to travel many miles to get to school. Louisa Dyer, whose husband Thomas Dyer manned Ohio's Marblehead Light, painted white marks on trees to designate the path from the station to the school so her kids could find the way. Ansel Knudson, the eleven-year-old son of Keeper Oscar H. Knudson of Door County's Cana Island Light, had a four-mile walk to school. One of Ansel's duties was to pick up the mail from the lighthouse mailbox on his way home. One day his mother went to the mailbox to send some letters she had forgotten to give Ansel that morning; there she found Ansel's shoes stuffed in the mailbox. When asked about it later, Ansel said he removed his shoes before going to school because none of the kids wore shoes, and he wanted to fit in. Beshoed or barefoot, keepers' kids were really just like kids everywhere.

Children at offshore stations had more difficulty getting an education, sometimes rowing across miles of water to get to school. Around the turn of the twentieth century, Ralph and Margaret Warner, whose father kept several lights on the St. Mary's River near the Soo Locks, had to carefully make their way across the top of the locks to their school on land. Sometimes, they had to crawl on their hands and knees to get across, as some sections of the locks had no hand railing. A keeper at Green Island Light in Ohio was said to have rigged up a dogsled team of Italian greyhounds to pull his children across the ice to school on shore.

At some stations, it was not possible for children to attend a school, and lighthouse parents taught their kids. At Turtle Island Light in Ohio the keeper's wife converted the second floor of the keeper's house into a one-

A propped-up ladder provides an afternoon of fun for the keepers' children at Minnesota's Split Rock Light, circa 1925. (Photo courtesy of Minnesota Historical Society)

room schoolhouse. The keeper's wife at Wisconsin's Potawatomi Light on Rock Island also schooled her kids at home. This arrangement was quite common at other isolated stations on the lakes.

The endless adventure of life on the Great Lakes fueled the spirit of lighthouse kids, who spent hours exploring the rocky shores and beaches near the station. Vivian DeRusha Quantz, whose father was keeper of Wisconsin's Devils Island Light, Michigan's Whitefish Point Light, and the stag station at Stannard Rock, wrote about her experiences in the book, *Foghorns Saved Lives, Too.* During her days as a lighthouse kid, Quantz passed the time searching for agates; her mother taught her how to distinguish the real agates from the millions of stones strewn along the shore. Quantz became fascinated with the natural world surrounding her, and she learned the names of the plants and flowers growing near the station. The sand dunes nearby also proved to be great fun. Quantz and her siblings would sled down the dunes on cardboard boxes in the summer.

Lighthouse life also offered limitless opportunities for mischief, and some youngsters got into a heap of trouble. During World War II, Anna, the daughter of Vern Bowen, Assistant Keeper of Passage Island Light on Lake Superior, built a campfire on the island with her siblings. The resulting fire smoldered but didn't flare up, so the kids decided to beef up their blaze with gasoline from the nearby spigot that lead to underground storage tanks. Predictably, the kids dripped a trail of gas from the spigot to the fire as they carried the gasoline, and a spark soon set the gasoline trail ablaze. When the flames reached the spigot, the storage tanks exploded, sending the kids scampering in every direction. Their mother ran from the keeper's house, screaming that the Japanese were bombing the island. Thankfully, no one was injured. Anna's father put out the fire, and, when the district inspector arrived with a replacement supply of petroleum, Anna's father forced Anna to explain what happened. A stern lecture from the inspector hammered home the message: Anna was never again to use the Coast Guard gasoline supply to enliven a campfire.

Of course, not all mischief ended in a spectacular explosion. Lois Aho lived at the Marquette Harbor Light in Michigan when her father Walter Aho, a Coast Guardsman, was stationed there. When one of Lois's friends swiped a cigar from her father, the girls hid in a stand of cedar trees near the end of the catwalk that lead to the nearby fog signal building and tried to smoke the cigar. Just as they lit up the stogie, their fathers came strolling along the catwalk, and one commented that he smelled cigar smoke. The girls extinguished their Havana in a hurry and managed to stay hidden until their fathers walked away. Lois and her friends swore off cigar smoking from that point on.

Great Lakes lighthouse kids needed to be on their best behavior during visits by the district inspector. But Vivian DeRusha Quantz had to shape up her act for the president of the United States. In the summer of 1928, President Calvin Coolidge visited Devils Island Light toward the end of his three-month vacation in northern Wisconsin. Vivian's brother Emmett sported a bow tie, and the girls wore dresses with ribbons to greet the president and the first lady. After a picnic lunch, President Coolidge told Head Keeper Hans F. Christensen that he would write a letter to the district inspector letting him know the lighthouse had passed his "presidential inspection" with flying colors.

Many Great Lakes lighthouse children helped their parents cut wood, shovel coal, plant gardens, haul supplies to the station from the tender ship, hunt, fish, cook, clean, and wash clothes. Most of the younger kids did not help with the official duties related to the light and were not allowed in the lantern room where fragile equipment was located. Even smudges from curious little hands could diminish the intensity of a station's Fresnel lens. But older children often helped their parents with official duties, from tending the light to staging a rescue of a stricken boat during the height of a storm. Sometimes, lighthouse children would grow up to become keepers themselves.

At some Great Lakes lighthouses, keeping the light became a family tradition, with several members of a single family tending beacons. The Garraty family included at least five keepers, beginning with Patrick Garraty, who took over as keeper of Michigan's Old Presque Isle Light in 1861. He would later become keeper of the new Presque Isle Light, built nearby in 1870, where he served until his retirement in 1885. His son Thomas then took over the head keeper's duties at Presque Isle Light, and he would remain in his position for fifty years. Thomas's brother Patrick served as an assistant keeper at Presque Isle. Patrick later became head keeper at the St. Clair Flats Range Lights on Lake St. Clair and at Middle Island Light near Presque Isle in Lake Huron. A third Garraty brother, John, worked at several Lake Huron lights and at the Mendota (Bete Grise) Light on Lake Superior, and a sister, Anna, kept the Presque Isle Harbor Range Lights from 1903 to 1926. By the time the younger Patrick retired in 1937, the Garraty family had served at Great Lakes stations over a span of seventy-six years.

Isolated on the Inland Seas

Although Great Lakes keepers kept themselves busy with work and hobbies, and many keepers lived with family, loneliness was never far away. When dangerous circumstances arose, keepers and their family members felt particularly isolated. Some keepers, especially young, single assistant keepers, had no companions with whom to idle away the long summer days. Friction between keepers at a station made loneliness more acute. Some lighthouses on the more inhospitable islands and shoals on the Lakes, such as Manitou Island Light on Lake Superior and Spectacle Reef Light on Lake Huron, were designated "stag stations," where only single male keepers could serve. Such stations were considered too

Established in 1870, the Mendota (Bete Grise) Light had a keeper until 1933. The restored fourth-order Fresnel lens in the tower, which dates to 1895, guided vessels into the Mendota Ship Canal until the light was deactivated in 1960.

dangerous for a keeper's family. Of course, they were very dangerous for the keepers themselves; underlying this policy was the belief that single male keepers who died on the job would not be missed as much as family men.

Keepers lived in close quarters at virtually every Great Lakes lighthouse, but at stag stations, particularly if a keeper didn't get along well with the other keepers, there seemed to be no breathing room. Stannard Rock Light in Lake Superior is the farthest lighthouse from land in the United States. The lighthouse lies twenty-three miles off a remote part of Michigan's Upper Peninsula coast and more than forty miles from Marquette, the nearest port. It is no wonder that those serving at the station nicknamed Stannard Rock "The Loneliest Place in the World." Before the Coast Guard took over the station in 1939, keepers there collected the highest pay of all U.S. lightkeepers, but the extra money didn't make up for the dreaded loneliness, nor did it lessen the inevitable conflicts between keepers. One keeper complained that no one at the station spoke to him for three weeks. When he threatened to swim ashore if the government didn't get him off Stannard Rock, the government transferred him to a different station. Later, a Coast Guardsman went mad at Stannard Rock, and he was removed from the station in a straightjacket. After an explosion at Stannard Rock in 1961 killed one Coast Guardsman and seriously injured another, the Lighthouse Board made the station fully automated. No more keepers would serve there—much to the relief of Coast Guardsmen across the Great Lakes.

The isolation got under the skin of some keepers. On July 4, 1876, the keeper of Wisconsin's Pilot Island Light, Victor E. Rohn, wrote in his log: "Independence day came in fine after a heavy southeast gale. This island affords about as much independence and liberty as Libby Prison, with the difference of guards in favor of this place, and chance of outside communication in favor of the other."

Mrs. Alexander McLean, wife of the keeper of the Raspberry Island Light in Wisconsin's Apostle Islands was a little more direct. "I hate lighthouses," she told a reporter in 1931. "They are so lonely. Going from one island to another . . . isn't much fun, especially when you have to go in a small boat and maybe get caught in a storm. We left Raspberry Island in 1916, and I was glad to see the last of it."

Unforeseen events deepened the sense of isolation. In the 1930s, the keeper of the Outer Island Light in the Apostles died at the station toward the end of the shipping season. The assistant keeper was the only other person around. He spent the next twelve days at the lighthouse with his dead boss until the tender ship arrived to take them off the island for the season.

In November 1883, the keeper of Passage Island Light near Isle Royale in Lake Superior left his wife and three children at the station when he went ashore for supplies. While he was away, a winter storm moved in, making a return trip to the station impossible. The keeper's family spent the whole winter on the island, with minimal provisions. They survived on whatever they could catch on the island or through the ice. When the keeper returned to the island in the spring of 1884, he found his family nearly starved to death—but alive.

For most Great Lakes lighthouse keepers and their families, miles of water, vast wilderness areas, and Mother Nature's mood swings left them utterly alone in the heart of North America. But most keepers were well aware of the conditions when they signed on to serve at a Great Lakes lighthouse. The majority of keepers made peace with their solitude and rolled with the punches. After all, the job may have been lonely, but the view was fabulous.

Rebuilt in 1904 after a storm destroyed the original in 1886, the Michigan City East Pierhead Light replaced the Old Michigan City Light.

CHAPTER 3

Lore of Lakes and Lights

Left: *The rough limestone tower of the existing Sodus Point Light served for just twenty-six years. Though dark for more than a century, the old sentinel still stands watch over the waters of Lake Ontario.*

Above: *The view of Lake Ontario from the tower of Sodus Point Light.*

To look at it one way, it is rather amazing that tender ships didn't sail out to Great Lakes light stations every month or so to pick up the dead bodies. Life on the Great Lakes was dangerous, both for those sailing the lakes and for those manning the beacons. Epic storms, ships foundering near lighthouses, terrified crews struggling for their lives, the occasional murder or suicide, and accidents involving lightkeepers have all become a part of Great Lakes history and lore. The sense of romance and mystery long attached to lighthouses has also given rise to tales of lighthouse spirits and other supernatural events. For the majority of Great Lakes lightkeepers, life was pretty mundane and routine most of the time. But some of the time, at some of the stations, things got a little out of hand.

Shipwrecks and Lightkeepers

When conditions are just right, storms strike the Great Lakes with little regard for the value of a ship's cargo or the sanctity of human life. Sometimes, when keepers were still working the lights for the season and ships sailed across the lakes trying to get one last load to port before navigation ended for the year, a cold wind would blow in from the Canadian plains. Slowly but steadily, the barometer would drop and the snow would start to fall. The waves would grow into towering white-capped peaks, transforming the landscape of the Great Lakes from a passive, watery plain into a maelstrom of boiling anger. Any vessel on the water when such a storm strikes may suddenly find herself in a battle for her life.

On September 2, 1905, Keeper John Irvine of the Outer Island Light in Wisconsin's Apostle Islands watched from the lantern room as bad weather began to brew on Lake Superior. As the wind howled and the rain razored down, Irvine noted the remarkably intense storm in his watchbook, describing it as "a [terrible] gale blowing from the NE, the biggest sea that I have seen" at the station. That afternoon, Keeper Irvine spotted a barge struggling in the high seas two miles to the northeast of the lighthouse. The barge, loaded with iron ore and bound for Chicago, was the *Pretoria*. The steamship *Venezuela* had been towing the barge, but the storm snapped the tow cable, leaving the *Pretoria* to fend for herself off Outer Island in the middle of a major gale.

As the keeper watched from the tower, a lifeboat left the *Pretoria*. Keeper Irvine scrambled down the lighthouse steps and out into the gale. From the shore Keeper Irvine could do nothing but watch as the approaching lifeboat capsized, tossing Captain Charles Smart and his nine crewmembers into Lake Superior. Some of the

crew managed to hang onto the overturned lifeboat, but five men never resurfaced after plunging into the lake.

As the turtled lifeboat and its weakened and half-frozen crew drifted toward the island, Keeper Irvine knew the men would not be able to pull themselves onto the rocky beach. He waded into the frigid water, steeling his resolve to do what had to be done. One by one, Keeper Irvine pulled the five survivors to shore.

After a hearty meal, the captain of the *Pretoria* and the remnants of his crew spent the night in Outer Island Light, resting under wool Lighthouse Board blankets near the potbellied stove. The next day the *Venezuela*, which had come looking for its barge and her crew after the storm had subsided, rescued the survivors.

That storm of early September also sank the *Sevona* near the Sand Island Light on the other side of the Apostles. And the gale was only one of two major gales to strike Lake Superior during the 1905 shipping season. In late November, not even three months later, the notorious Mataafa Blow struck. The storm, often called the worst storm ever to swoop down over the Great Lakes, was actually the second storm to strike Lake Superior in a matter of days. Because many ships had ventured out onto the lake again after the first storm, the toll in ships and lives after the second storm was very high. The devastating loss of lives and cargo along Minnesota's North Shore as a result of the Mataafa Blow lead in part to the establishment of the Split Rock Light five years later.

The first storm blew into Duluth on November 23, 1905, with heavy rains and strong winds. The winds had picked up to sixty miles per hour, and the rain had turned to slushy snow. The Coast Guard posted storm-warning flags early in the day, and captains—used to the late-November temper tantrums of Lake Superior—heeded the warnings and kept their ships in port. Despite the considerable strength of the storm, no lives were lost and shipping interests suffered little damage.

By November 25, the weather had calmed, settling into a typical post-storm pattern of fair skies and cold temperatures. As this was the end of the shipping season, the fair weather inspired a mad dash of ships across Lake Superior. Captains wanted to deliver their final cargo loads before the ports and waterways on and between the lakes started to freeze.

As late as the morning of November 27, 1905, weather forecasters predicted continued fair skies and cold temperatures. By that evening, snow began to fall in Duluth, and the winds quickly picked up to around forty miles per hour. By the following morning, winds were sustained above seventy miles per hour, and the

On September 2, 1905, a major gale swept into Lake Superior. The steamship Sevona *grounded on a shoal near the Sand Island Light in the Apostle Islands. The ship was one of two to go down in the Apostles that night.*

THE UNSINKABLE BUFFALO LIGHTSHIP

*T*hirteen miles west of Buffalo Harbor, on the Ontario coast of Lake Erie, a treacherous shoal stretches out from Point Abino. In the nineteenth century, the Lighthouse Board placed buoys in the water to mark the jagged reef. By the early years of the twentieth century, however, the Bureau of Lighthouses decided the area needed a more substantial aid to navigation, so they anchored a lightship over the shoal.

Lightship No. 82 was built at the Muskegon, Michigan, shipyard of the Racine-Truscott–Shell Lake Boat Company in the first half of 1912. The eighty-foot, steel-hulled vessel had a beam of twenty-one feet and room for six crewmen, including a tiny galley and sleeping quarters with slanted bunks that kept the crew safely in their beds during heavy seas. Up on deck, the lightship had a main lantern mast to the fore of the ship, supporting three kerosene-fueled lanterns. The vessel also had a ten-inch, steam-powered fog whistle.

On August 3, 1912, the Bureau of Lighthouses used four four-ton anchors to firmly position the lightship off of Point Abino. She was thereafter known as the *Buffalo Lightship*, due to her position on the approach to Buffalo Harbor. Although the lightship was stationed in Canadian waters, the U.S. Bureau of Lighthouses maintained the vessel. Captain Hugh M. Williams commanded the lightship and supervised the work of her five additional crewmembers.

At the time the *Buffalo Lightship* assumed her post, only one lightship—*Lightship No. 37*, stationed in the Atlantic off Five Fathom Bank, New Jersey—had sunk while on station in the United States. A hurricane brought down *Lightship No. 37* in August 1893. But most mariners on the Great Lakes considered freshwater lightships unsinkable. After all, the Great Lakes rarely had storms with wind speeds that approached hurricane strength. The lightships were specifically designed to stay afloat in rough weather. Lightships had flatter hulls than most boats and had bilge keels at the low point of the hull to inhibit rolling. Life on the *Buffalo Lightship* could be lonely and boring. Sometimes the swaying lightship induced widespread seasickness among her crew. But the men had little reason to fear for their lives. The *Buffalo Lightship* and her crew marked her shoal without event during the remainder of the 1912 shipping season and throughout 1913.

But on November 8, 1913, an unprecedented weather pattern would determine the *Buffalo Lightship*'s fate. That day, two low-pressure systems collided over Lake Superior, generating blizzard conditions. Mean-while, a third low-pressure system swept northward toward Lake Erie, producing high winds and tremendous snowfall. As the three fronts converged, the crew of the *Buffalo Lightship* found themselves directly in the path of a freshwater hurricane.

Lake Huron took the brunt of the storm on November 9, losing eight ships and 178 sailors. Another sixty men and two more ships would go down on the other lakes, including the *Buffalo Lightship* and her crew of six, which vanished without a trace.

In the early morning hours of November 11, the steamer *Champlain*, loaded with grain and battered from riding out the storm, passed Point Abino and noted the *Buffalo Lightship* was nowhere to be seen. Arriving at Buffalo, the captain of the *Champlain* dutifully reported the missing lightship. His report was not met with alarm, despite the magnitude of the storm. Officials assumed the lightship—which was, after all, unsinkable—had simply been blown off station.

But a cursory search around Point Abino revealed no lightship, and the inspector for the Tenth Lighthouse District, Roscoe House, became worried. The inspector ordered the launch of formal search vessels; he aided in the search on board the lighthouse tender *Crocus*.

Several days after the storm, a Buffalo resident was walking along the Lake Erie beach near the city, where he stumbled upon a life preserver inscribed with the words "Lightvessel No. 82," the first tangible clue that the lightship had gone down. Soon thereafter, another stroller found a piece of wood scrawled with the words "Good-by, Nellie, the ship is breaking up fast. Williams." The message was believed to have been a final note from Captain Williams to his wife. Several days later, the captain's body was found on the same beach.

The wreck of the *Buffalo Lightship* was not discovered until the following spring, and the Bureau of Lighthouses raised her in the fall of 1915. Though little more than the hull remained intact, the Bureau of Lighthouses completely rebuilt the lightship and sent her back into service as a relief ship and on station in Lake Michigan.

After the sinking of the *Buffalo Lightship*, a temporary lightship marked the shoal off Point Abino. Then, in 1917, the Canadian government established Point Abino Light onshore, finally marking the shoal with a relatively storm-proof lighthouse. The 1917 Point Abino Light still stands. And the "unsinkable" *Buffalo Lightship* remains the only American lightship ever to go down on the Great Lakes.

The Lighthouse Board built Minnesota's Two Harbors Light in 1892 to guide ore ships sailing in to and away from the ore docks at Two Harbors.

snow had buried cities and towns along the lake. Many, many ships were suddenly in a whole lot of trouble.

The Mataafa Blow gets its name from the steamship of the same name that struggled off the shore of Duluth during the height of the storm. On the afternoon of November 27, the *Mataafa* sailed out the Duluth Ship Canal with a barge, the *James Nasmyth*, in tow. Both vessels were loaded with iron ore, and Captain R. F. Humble of the *Mataafa*, like so many other captains across Lake Superior on that fateful day, observed fair skies and deemed it safe to set sail.

By the time the tandem ships were passing the Two Harbors Light and the Two Harbors East Breakwater Light on Minnesota's North Shore, the storm was upon them. The powerful steamer ground to a halt in eighty-mile-per-hour headwinds, and by the following morning, the captain realized further effort in the face of such wind was fruitless. Captain Humble ordered that the *Mataafa* return to Duluth, where they could wait out the storm. Through the blinding snow and rollick-

ing waves, the ships slowly turned around and steamed for Duluth with the wind at their backs.

Approaching the Duluth Ship Canal, the captain took stock of the rough seas and the narrow canal entrance. He quickly decided to cut the barge free as the pounding waves made it impossible to tow the *Nasmyth* safely into the harbor. The heavily loaded barge was anchored and cut loose. As it turned out, the *Nasmyth* would survive the storm, riding out the tempest anchored off the Duluth shoreline.

The *Mataafa* sailed toward the canal and safety. Indeed, Captain Humble reached the waterway entrance and ably steered her bow into the canal, the South Breakwater Inner and Outer Lights on his port side and the north breakwater, which didn't yet have a lighthouse, on the starboard side. But halfway into the refuge, a precipitous wave lifted the stern of the 5,000-ton steamship high in the air. The bow struck bottom, and then the whole ship smashed against the north breakwater. The ship's rudder was destroyed. Then, in one mighty surge, the waters of Lake Superior jerked the *Mataafa* out of the ship canal and dragged her back out onto the open lake. Unable to steer, Captain Humble and his crew just held on. A new round of large waves slammed the ship against the rocks along shore, cracking the *Mataafa* in half as easily as a kid breaks a stick over his knee. Although the *Mataafa* broke up just off the shore of a major port, Captain Humble and part of his crew spent the night huddled in the ship's bow, as a rescue crew could not reach the ship in such violent seas. A U.S. Life-Saving Service crew rescued those in the bow the following morning.

Unfortunately, the nine crewmen in the ship's aft portion died that night, either drowning or freezing to death in the icy waters of the lake. Some of the bodies actually froze to the *Mataafa* and later had to be chipped free.

During the height of the storm the blowing snow reduced visibility to near zero across Lake Superior. Minnesota's Arrowhead region on the North Shore of the lake was a particularly hazardous area even in good weather, as the iron deposits in the rock along the shore made ship compasses spin wildly. To make matters worse, the eighty-five miles of coastline that stretched between the North Shore towns of Grand Marais and Two Harbors had no lighthouses or fog signal stations at all. A half dozen ships would founder along this shoreline during the Mataafa Blow, including several vessels near Stony Point, the future site of Split Rock Light.

On the night of November 28, the steamer *William Edenborn* plied her way along the North Shore with the barge *Madeira* in tow. The hurricane-force winds drove the *Edenborn* off course, and the captain, unable to take compass readings, quickly found himself in dire straits. As was the case with many steamers and barges on Lake Superior during the storm, the thick cable towline that connected them snapped early the following morning, leaving each of the ships to fend for herself.

The captain of the *Edenborn* estimated his position based on the wind and gave the order for the ship to steam forward, figuring they would sail out a little from shore and drop anchor to ride out the storm. But within

This old fishing boat, located near Sturgeon Point Light on Lake Huron, is one of many vessels to be destroyed on the Great Lakes.

The Pointe Aux Barques Life-Saving Station once stood next to its namesake lighthouse. Today, the inactive station is on display several miles away in Huron City, Michigan.

a few minutes, the crew heard a tremendous scraping sound over the howling winds. The captain realized the *Edenborn* was driving right up into the North Shore forest rather than heading out into the lake. By then, it was too late for the huge steamer. With her bow beached in the woods near the Split Rock River, the great ship cracked in the middle and settled. The majority of the crew survived.

The *Madeira* drifted toward the shore as well, though her captain was equally confused about exactly where they were. Predictably, she also drove ashore, at the base of a cliff within a mile of the future site of Split Rock Light. One of the sailors aboard the *Madeira* leaped from the ship onto the rocks at the base of the cliff, and then slowly, painstakingly, clawed his way up the rock face, carrying a long rope. Once on top, he lowered the rope to the barge, which was starting to break up on the rocky shore, and helped eight men scale the cliff. Only one crewman drowned.

In all, twenty-nine ships sank or were damaged in the 1905 Mataafa Blow on Lake Superior. The North Shore carnage led to a campaign by the Lake Carriers' Association, a consortium of the owners of some five hundred lake freighters, to establish a lighthouse near where the *Madeira* had smashed on the rocks. In March 1907, the U.S. Congress agreed, appropriating $75,000 to build a lighthouse and a fog signal station at Stony Point. Split Rock Light, named after the area around the station, was lit for the first time in 1910.

Despite being rather obvious things for ships to avoid, many vessels have hit offshore lighthouses and the hazards they mark. On May 27, 1933, the *George M. Cox*

departed from Houghton, Michigan, bound for Port Arthur, Ontario (now part of Thunder Bay, Ontario), on northern Lake Superior. The passenger ship had originated in Chicago and was traveling to the Canadian town to pick up tourists and carry them back to Chicago for the Century of Progress Exposition. A large contingent of Chicago passengers was aboard the northbound ship enjoying a late spring cruise. The *George M. Cox's* route would take her northwest around the far western tip of Isle Royale and then northeast into the port. Along her route, she would round the 130-foot tall Rock of Ages Light, which stands on a serrated reef off the western end of Isle Royale.

The *George M. Cox* steamed along on the foggy night of May 23, approaching the western edge of Isle Royale around dinnertime. Some of the Rock of Ages keepers were in the lantern room as the ship approached, but they did not see the vessel's lights due to the fog. However, as the ship drew nearer, one of the keepers spotted the masts of the *Cox* poking above the fog bank. The ship seemed to be on a collision course with the lighthouse. The keepers attempted to attract the attention of the *Cox's* crew by repeatedly blasting the foghorn and flashing the lighthouse lamp.

The ship, however, didn't slow or change course. To the keepers' horror and to the supping passengers' shock, the *George M. Cox* plowed into the Rock of Ages Reef, just missing the lighthouse, at an estimated speed of seventeen knots. The force of impact as the steamship drove high up on the reef sent champagne flutes, bow-tied waiters, suitcases, and nattily dressed passengers flying.

Passengers and crew scrambled in the aftermath trying to get to the deck to find out what had happened. The keepers of Rock of Ages made their way along the reef to the *Cox* to aid passengers. The crew of the ship launched the lifeboats and lowered many passengers safely to the water. Though it was foggy that night, the lake itself was calm. Only four passengers had been seriously hurt by the impact. A passing freighter, the *Morris B. Tremaine*, picked up the critically injured and took them on to Port Arthur for treatment.

The remaining 118 passengers and crew spent the night on Rock of Ages Reef. The lighthouse wasn't big enough to harbor all of the castaways, so the survivors took turns standing inside. The next morning a Coast Guard cutter picked up the bedraggled, chilled-to-the-bone survivors and carried them back to Houghton.

The *George M. Cox* remained stranded on Rock of

Psychics visiting Michigan's Big Bay Point Light on Lake Superior have identified five distinct ghosts inhabiting the lighthouse, which today serves as a bed-and-breakfast.

Ages Reef for some time. Eventually, waves stirred up by a heavy storm dislodged the battered ship. She slipped from her perch on the reef, and, with a gaping gash in her hull, she promptly sank.

Morbid Lights

Squaw Island Light, near the top of Lake Michigan, nine miles northwest of St. James Harbor on Beaver Island, is a cold, lonely, and forbidding place. The once-elegant 1892 lighthouse was abandoned after it was deactivated in 1928, and the seventy-plus years of neglect are quite apparent today. But in December 1900, the lighthouse was bustling with activity as Keeper William H. Shields and Assistant Keepers Owen J. McCauley and Lucien F. Morden worked to close the station for the season. After the work was completed, the keepers and Shields's wife and niece climbed into a small sailboat for the trip to St. James Harbor where they would spend the winter.

The cold wind blew steadily out of the northeast, catching the sail and powering the boat toward St. James Harbor. But a sudden gust from the northwest swooped into the sail, tipping the small boat over and dumping the five passengers into the December waters. All managed to stay close to the overturned boat, but there was not enough room for any of the five to pull themselves completely out of the lake. The keepers helped the two women tether themselves to the boat with the sailboat's riggings, but all remained drenched and partially submerged in the frigid lake.

Slowly, the cold crept into the bodies and minds of the five that night. Shivering affected all of them almost immediately and eventually escalated to convulsions. The keeper's niece, strapped to the hull, was said to sing a shaky hymn as night fell, but her soft voice fell silent just after the sun went down, and she died soon thereafter.

A short while later, the keeper's wife begged to be cut loose from her tether, too cold and tired to hang on any longer. Things seemed hopeless for all as the turtled boat and its four remaining passengers slowly drifted through the December night. To relieve his wife's suffering, Keeper Shields granted her request and cut her free; she quickly slipped under the waves. Assistant Keeper Morden soon gave in to the cold as well, sliding into the water shortly after Mrs. Shields went under.

Keeper Shields and Assistant Keeper McCauley survived the night on the overturned boat and clung to life

SURFMEN ON THE INLAND SEAS

*I*n the early days of lighthouses on the Great Lakes, lightkeepers were responsible for rescuing crews from sinking vessels. Stories of heroic keepers rescuing sailors in grave danger make up a significant amount of Great Lakes history. But as shipping increased on the lakes, the need for a formal organization in charge of rescuing sailors in peril became apparent. In 1876, the United States Life-Saving Service hit the lakes, and a new set of heroes assumed their posts.

"Surfmen," such as these men from the Evanston Life-Saving Service station in Illinois, manned lifesaving stations across the Great Lakes. The stations were often placed near lighthouses. (Photo courtesy of the Evanston Historical Society)

In the first year, workers built a total of twenty stations with stations located on every lake except Lake Superior. The following year, the service added ten more, including four on Lake Superior. To take advantage of existing infrastructure such as piers and boathouses, the service built many of the lifesaving stations near lighthouses. And because the lighthouses stood on prominent points or headlands with good views of the water or at particularly dangerous areas where wrecks were more common, lighthouse locations made great sites for lifesaving service stations.

The service divided the thirty initial stations into two classes. First-class stations, usually in remote locations, had a full-time crew and were completely equipped. First-class lifesaving stations on the lakes included the Big Sandy Creek station near the Stony Point Light on Lake Ontario, the Pointe Aux Barques station next to the lighthouse of the same name on Lake Huron, and the Crisp Point station near the Crisp Point Light on Lake Superior. Usually located near towns and staffed by volunteers, second-class stations, also known as lifeboat stations, included the Oswego station near the Oswego West Pierhead Light on Lake Ontario, the Fairport station near the Old Fairport Main (Grand River) Light on Lake Erie, and the Two Rivers Station near the Two Rivers North Pierhead Light on Lake Michigan. The service continued to add lifesaving stations as needed. By 1893, the Great Lakes had forty-seven stations. By 1900, the number had risen to sixty.

The lifesaving stations each had a resident keeper in charge of all operations, including the supervision of a crew of six to eight "surfmen"—the nickname for the workers of the U.S. Life-Saving Service. During the shipping season at first-class stations, the keeper and the surfmen remained at or near the station keeping watch in the lookout tower or patrolling the beach with an eye to the lake for vessels in distress.

During rescue operations, the surfmen used specially designed rescue boats that featured a wide beam for stability, a keel made of iron to keep the boat upright, and a self-bailing apparatus to prevent capsizing. Nearly every Great Lakes station also had a Lyle gun, a cannon that fired a cast-iron projectile attached to a shotline. When seas were too high for the launch of a rescue boat and the shipwreck was within six hundred yards of shore, surfmen used the Lyle gun, firing the projectile over the wreck and securing the shotline coiled in a particular way so it would unfurl with ease. Surfmen then connected a breeches buoy—a round life preserver with an attached support apparatus that resembled a pair of pants—to the shotline and wheeled it out to the ship. Each sailor would then ride back to shore dangling inside the breeches buoy.

On Halloween night in 1878, the Grand Haven Life-Saving Station crew on Lake Michigan and the keepers of the White River Light attempted such a rescue, although things hardly went by the book. That night, the sailing ship *L.C. Woodruff*, loaded with midwestern corn, encountered high seas and howling winds along the eastern shore of Lake Michigan. In the early evening, when it was clear the ship would be unable to reach a harbor of refuge before dark, the captain of the *Woodruff* ordered the shipmen to drop anchor about a half mile out from the White River Light. Heavy winds and rough seas badly battered the square-rigged vessel that night, shredding her sails and snapping several of her masts.

Watching from the lighthouse, Keeper William Robinson fretted over the fate of the *Woodruff*. Grand Haven, the nearest lifesaving station, was forty miles away, and the tumultuous storm showed no signs of subsiding. Overnight, the strong winds began to pull the *Woodruff* along shore, dragging the anchor along with the stricken ship. As the *Woodruff* approached shore near the lighthouse, she struck bottom and began to break up, sending her crew scampering up the rigging. Soon, the anchor chain snapped. The wind dragged the partially submerged ship another half mile up the shore.

In the morning, Keeper Robinson sent his son Thomas, who was also an assistant keeper, across sheltered White Lake to town to telegraph the Grand Haven Life-Saving Station for help. While they waited for the official rescuers, the keeper and several men attempted to reach the *Woodruff* in a small boat, but the high seas made a rescue in such a small craft impossible. Within minutes of pushing off the beach, the ragtag rescue team found themselves dumped into the lake, their boat overturned by the waves.

Meanwhile, the Grand Haven lifesavers responded to the telegram, sending five men and a Lyle gun by train. The lifesavers arrived in Whitehall, near the lighthouse, on November 1 at one o'clock in the afternoon. Assistant Keeper Thomas Robinson met the train and led the rescuers to the stricken ship.

Once on the beach, the surfmen could clearly see the wind-battered crew of the *Woodruff* dangling from the remaining masts. The lifesaving team fired the Lyle gun, attempting to attach a shotline to the *Woodruff*'s riggings. After a few tries, they connected a line to the ship. Keeping a tight grip on the line, the rescue crew climbed into a small boat and shoved off from the beach, with Assistant Keeper Tom Robinson and several surfmen aboard. Although they intended to steadily pull themselves out to the vessel, the waves were too big for the boat, and before long the vessel was swamped.

Four members of the *Woodruff*'s crew became impatient and decided to take matters into their own hands. They leaped from the riggings and grabbed the line that stretched to shore. The rope snapped, and the rescuers on shore started to pull, dragging the four men and the rescue crew whose boat had sunk all the way to the beach. One of the four *Woodruff* crewmembers would die the next day, but the others survived the ordeal. Four more men, including the captain of the ship, made it to shore by holding onto debris from the wreck and floating inland. Two of the crew had drowned during the disastrous storm.

In the end, the ship and its cargo were a total loss, but the rescue team, under the trying conditions, had saved most of the crew. Such dramatic rescues were commonplace for surfmen at Great Lakes lifesaving stations. Heroism was just part of the job.

all the next morning. A passing steamship finally rescued the barely alive keepers the following afternoon. The men had been in the water for nearly twenty-four hours.

The Coast Guard recovered the bodies of the two women and gave them a proper burial ashore. Assistant Keeper Morden's body was not found. The incident left Keeper Shields partially paralyzed, and he had to have one of his legs amputated. He later worked for the Lighthouse Board at the Charlevoix Supply Depot. Assistant Keeper McCauley suffered frostbite, but he recovered and went on to become head keeper at Squaw Island and later at the St. Joseph North Pier Lights.

At some stations, tragedies seemed to happen with regularity. Granite Island's James Wheatley endured the deaths of multiple associates and family members during his service at the Lake Superior lighthouse from 1885 to 1915. In 1898, his son William was sailing to Granite Island in a small boat when a sudden squall overturned his craft, drowning the young man. Five years later, as Assistant Keeper John McMartin sailed away from the station bound for Marquette, Keeper Wheatley watched a wave strike the boat, causing it to capsize. The waves quickly swept McMartin against the island's rocky shore. Battered, he soon slipped under the surface and drowned.

Family members were often the most vulnerable of lighthouse residents. At Wisconsin's Chambers Island Light, Assistant Keeper Sam Hanson endured the death of his wife in 1915. In 1921, his son Edgar died from appendicitis. The keepers couldn't get the sixteen-year-old to a hospital in Sturgeon Bay in time to save him. The following spring, Assistant Keeper Hanson's other son Clifford, age eighteen, walked across the ice toward Fish Creek to get the mail. He broke through the ice near the Eagle Bluff Light and soon succumbed to the cold and drowned. Eagle Bluff Keeper Peter Coughlin saw the accident, but he could do nothing to save the young man. Assistant Keeper Hanson remained in the lighthouse service thereafter, but he was plagued by crippling bouts of depression for the rest of his life.

Even mundane injuries or sicknesses could turn tragic if the person didn't reach a hospital or clinic in time. Despite their remote location, lightkeepers and their families were in no way immune to the diseases—typhoid fever, scarlet fever, tuberculosis, and influenza—that swept through America in the days before immunizations, penicillin, and other medical treatments were available.

At the close of the shipping season in 1899, Gull Rock Keeper John Nolen and his family moved ashore to Calumet, Michigan, so seven-year-old son Jamie could attend school. One day in January 1900, Jamie came home from school complaining of a sore throat and a headache. By the following morning, Jamie was running a high fever and had great difficulty swallowing his breakfast. That evening, the boy's body was covered with red spots, and the family summoned a doctor. The doctor diagnosed scarlet fever, and the Nolen's Calumet home was quarantined. The doctor instructed Mrs. Nolen to massage vapor rub onto Jamie's throat and chest and soak the boy in hot water to soothe the pain. Despite her efforts, Jamie died a few days later. Horribly, one month later, the Nolen's three-year-old daughter Violet also succumbed to the disease. Jamie and Violet's parents returned to Gull Rock Light in April 1900 childless and devastated.

Violence, although rare, also flared up at a few Great Lakes light stations. Perhaps it was the isolation that drove people to commit murder or suicide. In 1880, Assistant Keeper John Boyce, who served at Wisconsin's Pilot Island Light, killed himself at the station by slashing his jugular vein. Rumors abound as to what led to the eccentric loner's suicide, ranging from the loneliness of his assignment to despair over a failed love affair.

Other times keepers lashed out at one another. In June 1908, Keeper George Genry of the Grand Island Old North Light on Lake Superior sailed to Munising for provisions and to visit his wife, who lived in town. Keeper Genry had a reputation of being difficult to work with, and assistant keepers under his command moved to other posts with great frequency. Assistant Keeper Edward Morrison, who had just come to the island station two months earlier, operated the station while the keeper was ashore. Keeper Genry returned to the station on June 6.

Two days later, Keeper Thomas Irvine at Au Sable Point Light (called the Big Sable Light at the time) spotted a small rowboat drifting near his lighthouse, twenty-seven miles from the Grand Island Old North Light. Launching the station's boat, Keeper Irvine sailed out to the craft where he discovered the battered body of Assistant Keeper Edward Morrison sprawled in the bottom of the boat.

Munising officials sailed out to Grand Island to tell Keeper Genry of the tragic death of his assistant, but the officials found the station abandoned and a second station sailboat missing. That boat was later found tied ashore at a pier near Munising. The keeper was never to be heard from again.

Many speculated that Keeper Genry and Assistant Keeper Morrison had gotten into an argument, and that Genry had killed Morrison and set him adrift. Keeper Genry then had fled, perhaps disappearing into Canada. What really happened at the Grand Island Old North Light that June day will never be known, though circumstantial evidence certainly suggests Keeper Genry was one of the few Great Lakes keepers with a murderous heart.

Spirit Lights

According to the testimonies of credible witnesses, dozens of Great Lakes lighthouses are haunted. In 1961, the government transferred the navigational beacon from Big Bay Point Light on Lake Superior to a small steel tower nearby. In the 1980s, when the old lighthouse was used as a bed-and-breakfast, the owner of the bed-and-breakfast was in the keeper's house when he heard a clamorous banging outside. When he went outside to find out what the ruckus was about, the banging stopped and the owner saw nothing out of the ordinary. He went back inside, and it started again. The mysterious cacophony continued this pattern for awhile, thoroughly confusing the otherwise clear-minded owner.

Soon thereafter, a cleaning woman at the bed-and-breakfast reported someone in the downstairs shower, a bathroom that no guests would have been using. A check of the bathroom revealed nobody washing up, despite the housekeeper's insistence that she had heard something. A few days later, guests at the station saw a man walking across the grounds wearing a uniform that fit the description of the keeper's uniform during the period of the Lighthouse Board. Before they could get outside to see who it was, the man disappeared.

Later, psychics visited the lighthouse and made contact with the spirits at the station. They determined that one of the ghosts was likely the spirit of Keeper William Prior, who killed himself in 1901 after his son died from an infected wound. Another spirit told a psychic she was the ghost of a woman who had died at the lighthouse in the 1950s when the station was automated and sat abandoned. This spirit was very angry, saying she was incensed because she had died at the station, and no one knew what happened to her. Psychics could not

Above: *In 1989, the caretaker of the Old Fairport Main (Grand River) Light discovered she shared the old station with a feline ghost.*

Left: *Keeper Thomas Irvine, stationed at the Au Sable Point Light nearly thirty miles away from the Grand Island Old North Light, found the body of Grand Island Old North Light's Assistant Keeper Edward Morrison drifting in a rowboat.*

Above: *The Old Presque Isle Light on Lake Huron at Presque Isle, Michigan, was built for $5,000 in 1840. In 1992, Lorraine Parris, the caretaker of the old station, attempted to go outside during a storm, but the door was stuck. Moments later, lightning struck the ground outside where she would have been standing. Parris believes the spirit of her late husband George saved her life that day. This image has been digitally enhanced.*

Right: *In 1979, the light at Old Presque Isle turned itself on and the fourth-order Fresnel lens in the tower began to rotate.*

For years lightkeepers pulled open this door to climb the light tower at Old Presque Isle Light. After the light in the inactive tower began inexplicably to shine anew, the Coast Guard disconnected the power to the lantern room and removed the rotation gears.

But in 1992, the tower lit up again. Boaters, fishermen, pilots, and freighter captains all saw the phantom light. Rumors persisted that a spirit was climbing the tower stairs every night to tend the lamp.

determine the ghost's identity, but they were able to differentiate a total of five different ghosts at the bed-and-breakfast. Sightings continue with relative frequency to this day.

One of the most famous ghosts on the Great Lakes was said to reside at the abandoned Waugoshance Light in northern Lake Michigan, deactivated in 1912. John Herman came to Waugoshance Light as a second assistant keeper in 1887, rising to head keeper by 1890. Known for his fondness of liquor and practical jokes, Keeper Herman was well liked by those under his command at the lonely station.

In 1901, a tipsy Keeper Herman played a joke on one of the assistant keepers by locking him in the lantern room. The drunken keeper then stumbled down to the pier, fell into Lake Michigan, and quickly drowned.

Thereafter, the crew at Waugoshance Light reported some peculiar happenings. Chairs were kicked out from under crewmembers, empty coal buckets were found a short while later heaped with coal, and heavy doors would swing open and shut when the winds were calm. Finally, in 1912, the nearby White Shoal Light replaced the Waugoshance Light, and the rattled keepers could finally get away from the playful and inebriated ghost of John Herman.

On Lake Huron, both the Old Presque Isle Light and the nearby Presque Isle Light are said to be haunted. The Old Presque Isle Light was deactivated in 1871. Eventually, the Stebbins family became owners of the old station, restoring the lighthouse and opening it to the public as a museum. In 1977, George and Lorraine Parris took over as caretakers of the lighthouse.

George and Lorraine maintained the inactive station for many years, but in 1992, George passed away. Lorraine stayed on at the museum after the death of her husband—it was then that all of the mysterious happenings started. Later in 1992, Lorraine was returning to the lighthouse from the other side of Presque Isle Harbor when she saw a glow coming from the lantern room of the lighthouse. She brought a couple of friends to the spot where she saw the glow, and they saw the light as well. The light in the tower made no sense, as the power to the lantern room had been disconnected back in 1979, leaving nothing to be lit up. The floodlights highlighting the tower were turned off, the bulb in the lens apparatus was removed, and the lens was covered with a tarp, but townspeople still reported the glow every night. According to Lorraine Parris, the strange phenomenon continues to this day.

Lorraine also relates a story of a near-death experience at the station in 1992. A strong thunderstorm struck the peninsula that night, and when Lorraine tried to open the back door of the lighthouse so she could go outside to move her car into a more sheltered spot, she couldn't open the door. She later found two white chairs propped against the outside of the door to pin it shut. While she was trying to open the door, a bolt of lightning struck outside right where Lorraine would have been had the door opened freely. The strange occurrences at Old Presque Isle Light cannot be explained, but Lorraine stays on at the lighthouse, believing the spirit of her late husband is watching out for her.

The "new" Presque Isle Light also has a resident spirit. Just a mile away from the Old Presque Isle Light, the 113-foot tower took over the navigational duties after it was built in 1871. On certain nights, when the wind whips up and a storm settles in on the station, the sound of a woman wailing can be clearly heard above the gusts and rain.

The forlorn woman may be the ghost of a keeper's wife who was said to have gone mad at the station. Legend has it that the keeper locked her in a tunnel under the station where, tormented by her madness, she screamed until her death.

In another version of the story, the keeper was having an affair with a townswoman. He brought his mistress out to the Presque Isle Light and locked his wife in the tower while he committed his infidelities. The screaming is the tortured wailing of a woman betrayed.

A less bloodcurdling spirit is said to live at the Old Fairport Main (Grand River) Light in Ohio. In 1989, the resident caretaker of the lighthouse, which also houses a maritime museum, was peeling potatoes in the kitchen when she saw something small skitter by. Looking down the hall, she saw a gray kitten that seemed almost transparent. Oddly, the cat had no feet, yet the kitten hurried away and out of sight.

Over the next few months, the caretaker repeatedly saw the kitten-ghost, and at one point, even balled up a sock and played with it. The feline pounced after the ball when the caretaker tossed the sock over the cat or across the room.

The caretaker researched the history of the light station, and although there were many cats who lived there during the lighthouse's years of operation, one kitten stood out. In 1871, Joseph Babcock became keeper of the lighthouse, a man destined to spend many years at the light station. At one point during his years of service, his wife became ill and was bedridden for several months. While she was recovering, she played with a gray kitten, tossing a soft ball for the kitten to chase after and retrieve. The history records were unclear as to whether the cat died young.

Since the ghost kitty wasn't talking, the caretaker couldn't be certain that Mrs. Babcock's companion was her transparent, footless feline. Despite the uncertainty of its history, the playful ghost appeared to be trapped in a happy place, delighting a lighthouse caretaker as much as a century after its death.

A spirit wearing an old-fashioned dress with an apron has been spotted at Michigan's Pointe Aux Barques Light. The identity of the ghostly homemaker has not been determined.

CHAPTER 4

The Lighthouses of the Great Lakes: Changing with the Times

Left: *Lake Superior's Crisp Point Light looks a little lonely today in its remote corner of Michigan. Upon establishment in 1904, the site had a lifesaving station and quarters, keeper's house, fog signal building, oil house, two barns, boathouse and landing, and a tramway. The Coast Guard tore down most of the station after deactivation, and now only the tower and a small service room at its base remain.*

Above: *The National Park Service is restoring Lake Superior's Au Sable Point Light in Michigan, which stands within Pictured Rocks National Lakeshore. In this photograph, workers paint the tower.*

The twentieth century marked a complete makeover for Great Lakes lighthouses. Technological improvements, changes in the lighthouse administration system, reconstruction of some older lights, deactivation of others, and automation of every Great Lakes light all took place during this time. Despite such drastic changes, more than 200 of the 312 stations remaining in U.S. and Canadian waters still serve as active aids to navigation. Other lighthouses have become museums, bed-and-breakfasts, and tourist attractions. Most of the old lighthouses have been preserved, but sadly a few are threatened by erosion or are slowly succumbing to the harsh weather battering them year after year, to natural disasters such as fire and tornadoes, and to senseless acts of vandalism.

The Mechanics of Automation and the Earliest Automated Lights on the Lakes

The transformation of Great Lakes lighthouses began in the early years of the twentieth century. The first automated light on the Great Lakes was the Charity Island Light in Michigan's Saginaw Bay, which was built in 1857 and automated in 1900. Slowly, automation crept across the Great Lakes region, and five more Great Lakes lighthouses were automated before 1930.

Technological improvements played a major role in Great Lakes lighthouse automation. The dissolved acetylene gas burner, invented in 1906 by Nils Gustav Dalén, was one of the earliest inventions that led to wider automation. Dalén's device, which had a mantle similar to the light source in modern camping lanterns, vaporized the gas, allowing it to burn much more brightly. Dalén also invented the sun-valve, a nifty device that worked with the acetylene gas burner to automatically turn the light on and off. A specially coated metal rod with light-absorbing qualities was attached to the lever that controlled gas flow to the burner. As the sun rose in the morning, the rod absorbed the sunlight, heated up, and expanded, triggering the lever and turning off the gas flow to extinguish the light. Similarly, the rod contracted as the sun lowered in the evening, turning the beacon back on. The sun-valve had an advantage over timed switches also in use in lighthouses by this time: The sun-valve turned the beacon on not only at night, but also during mist, fog, and heavy cloud cover—conditions under which mariners needed a beacon.

The Bureau of Lighthouses installed Dalén's burner and sun-valve system in Wisconsin's Baileys Harbor Range Lights in 1923 and Green Island Light, also in Wisconsin, in 1935. The keepers at the nearby Cana Island Light maintained the lights at Baileys Harbor. They stopped by monthly to clean the lenses and refill the gas tanks, and they would head to the station immediately if there was any sign of trouble. Similarly, the keepers at Sherwood Point Light in Door County maintained the Green Island Light across Green Bay fourteen miles to the southeast.

Some Great Lakes lighthouses were automated using another trigger mechanism: the astronomical clock. This switching device automatically adjusted based on daylight hours as the season progressed, and a sun-valve served as a backup if conditions became too dark during the daytime. Peshtigo Reef Light, built in Green Bay in 1934 to replace a lightship in place there since 1906, always used this system—it was never manned. As with the Green Island Light, the keepers at Sherwood Point Light maintained this station. They were able to operate the fog signal remotely by radio.

Electricity, which is used to light every lighthouse on the Great Lakes today, was slow to catch on in the lighthouse service. The Lighthouse Board first tested an electric arc lamp in 1886 as an aid to navigation in the Statue of Liberty in New York Harbor. But it wasn't until after 1916, as the U.S. electrical network fanned out across the country and cheap generators were developed, that electricity started to power some Great Lakes lights. The more remote stations on the lakes, those far from power lines such as West Sister Island Light on Lake Erie and Skillagalee (Ile Aux Galets) Light on northern Lake Michigan, could not be powered without newly developed generators. Electrification really took off in the 1920s, and by the 1940s, the majority of Great Lakes lighthouses were electrified.

It was also during this time that lighthouse keepers began to use radio as a navigational system and as a way to control the operations of lighthouses. During World War I, the U.S. Department of Commerce and the Navy conducted experiments with electromagnetic radio waves. They discovered that when radio waves struck a coil of wire at a certain angle, electricity flowed through the coil, but if the waves struck the coil more directly, no electricity was produced. The Bureau of Standards in the Department of Commerce developed a device that could determine the direction from which the radio waves originated. At the same time, the Navy established a Morse code system to identify the source of the radio

As lighthouse automation spread across the Great Lakes, keepers at some stations took over the responsibility of maintaining nearby automated lights. After the Bureau of Lighthouses automated the Baileys Harbor Range Lights in 1923, the keepers at Wisconsin's Cana Island Light, pictured here, maintained them.

No longer active, the Rock Island Light in the St. Lawrence River is today owned by the New York State Office of Parks, Recreation and Historic Preservation.

Keepers at Wisconsin's Sherwood Point Light maintained the beacons at the Green Island Light and the Peshtigo Reef Light.

wave. Soon thereafter, the Navy installed such radio beacons on their ships and the Bureau of Lighthouses placed them in some light stations.

On the Great Lakes, *Lightship No. 103*, later re-named the *Lightship Huron*, stationed on Gray's Reef in northern Lake Michigan became the first light sta-tion to demonstrate a radio beacon in 1925, transmit-ting a radio signal of three long dashes. Ships receiving this signal could immediately identify the source as the lightship and tell precisely which direction the signal was coming from, which aided their navigation. Later, vessels could even estimate their distance from a Great Lakes light station. Lighthouses would transmit a radio signal and blow the foghorn at exactly the same time. The radio signal would reach a boat instantaneously while the audible fog signal would travel through air at a rate of one mile in five seconds. A mariner would mea-sure the time between the signals on a stopwatch and would then simply divide by five to determine the esti-mated distance of his vessel from the light station. By

1942, there were fifty-eight radio beacon stations operat-ing in American waters on the Great Lakes.

Radio beacons had several advantages over lighted beacons and fog signals. For starters, the signal could travel much farther than the luminous range of a light-house lamp or the audible range of a station's fog signal, making radio beacons particularly useful in foggy weather and for boats far out on the big lakes. And, unlike fog-horns, radio beacons were silent, a pleasant change for people living near a signal station.

Over time, some stations on the lakes received radio-broadcasting facilities. In 1935, Wisconsin's Sherwood Point Light became the first in the country to receive such an installation. The Sherwood Point keeper broadcasted two daily weather reports from the keeper's house.

Some other Great Lakes stations had radiotele-phones. Each station was to contact a shore station at an allotted time to check-in and pass on any non-emergency news such as weather conditions. If an emergency arose, these stations could telephone a short-wave radio operator who would then contact the shore station or district headquarters. In 1937, the Bureau of Lighthouses began broadcasting "Notices to Mariners Regarding Aids to Navigation" by radiotelephone from Sault Ste. Marie. The broadcast provided information about problems with lighthouses and buoys, weather conditions, and more. The next year, five other broadcasting stations went on the air across the Great Lakes.

Radio signals were also used on the Great Lakes to automatically turn lighthouses on and off using the coil system. Some Great Lakes lighthouses, such as the Fourteen Foot Shoal Light, established in 1930 in northern Lake Huron, had this system from their inception and were never manned. Keepers at the nearby Poe Reef Light monitored Fourteen Foot Shoal Light.

One of the most significant later developments that affected Great Lakes lighthouses was the solar-powered battery, first used in lighthouses in the 1960s. Today, solar power is nearly universal at the more remote Great Lakes light stations, as well as at some that aren't all that remote, given the economical benefits of free electricity. Today, solar panels are clearly visible bolted to the railing around the lantern rooms at stations such as Poverty Island Light in northern Lake Michigan, Gull Rock Light in Lake Superior, and Wisconsin's Sheboygan Breakwater Light on Lake Michigan.

The Bureau of Lighthouses

While all of this technological change began to affect Great Lakes lighthouses, the administration of American lighthouses also changed for the first time since 1852. On June 17, 1910, the government dissolved the Lighthouse Board and established a new Bureau of Lighthouses within the united Department of Commerce and Labor (after 1913, the Bureau was under the newly created Department of Commerce). The government pulled the military from lighthouse duties and again placed control of America's lighthouses into the hands of one person, Superintendent of Lighthouses George R. Putnam.

Putnam was perhaps a surprising choice given his background. But in reality, Putnam was tapped to run the Bureau of Lighthouses in much the same way keepers had obtained their positions until 1896: He had connections. A longtime employee of the Coast and Geodetic Survey, a government organization charged with mapping seaside territory, Putnam assumed the post of director of coast surveys in the Philippines, then a U.S. territory, back in 1900. While in the Far East, Putnam made the acquaintance of the governor of the islands, one William Howard Taft. After Taft assumed the presidency of the United States in 1909, he asked Putnam to lead his newly created Bureau of Lighthouses.

Putnam was skeptical of taking the position at first.

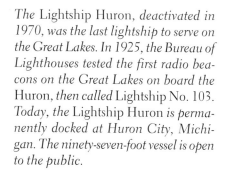

The Lightship Huron, *deactivated in 1970, was the last lightship to serve on the Great Lakes. In 1925, the Bureau of Lighthouses tested the first radio beacons on the Great Lakes on board the* Huron, *then called* Lightship No. 103. *Today, the* Lightship Huron *is permanently docked at Huron City, Michigan. The ninety-seven-foot vessel is open to the public.*

Fourteen Foot Shoal Light, in northern Lake Huron near Cheboygan State Park, was automatically operated using a radio coil system. The keepers at the nearby Poe Reef Light controlled the station and regularly stopped by for maintenance.

He worried that his mapmaking background wasn't sufficient training to run the Bureau of Lighthouses and thought that political changes, such as a change in the White House administration, might later undermine his position. But he decided to accept Taft's offer anyway, making the quality of America's lighthouses his top priority. As Putnam wrote in his 1937 autobiography *Sentinels of the Coasts: The Log of a Lighthouse Engineer:* "[My] main purpose throughout the years was to avoid the political shoals in order to give the navigators the best protection against the marine shoals."

Like Stephen Pleasonton, Putnam was interested in administering America's lighthouses economically. But unlike Pleasonton, he was dedicated to administering an effective, safe Bureau of Lighthouses. Putnam balanced economy and safety through efficient use of resources and decentralization of power.

Putnam encouraged keepers to stretch every last bit of life out of their supplies, from paintbrushes to furniture. Evidence of uselessness had to be demonstrated

and the item turned over to the inspector before items would be replaced. Careful rationing of critical supplies, such as kerosene, coal, and paint, was also a big concern for keepers, as the Bureau allotted such items based on the previous year's inventory.

Putnam also worked to decentralize the Bureau. Although the number of aids to navigation in the United States doubled during his twenty-five years of service, Putnam reduced the number of employees in the Bureau's Washington office. Putnam gave district superintendents the job of supervising operations because local representatives could respond more quickly and efficiently to mariners' and lightkeepers' requests.

Putnam also focused on improving the benefits and financial rewards for keepers across the service. He convinced Congress to enact the General Lighthouse Act of June 20, 1918, which, for the first time, extended pension benefits to lighthouse keepers. Under his watch, Congress also extended health benefits and disability insurance to keepers in 1916 and expanded disability

Lake Superior's Sand Hills Light, one of the few lighthouses established after George Putnam took office in 1910, was first lit in 1919 and is an elegant bed-and-breakfast today.

insurance in 1925. By the end of the 1920s, salaries also grew substantially. When Putnam stepped down in 1935, he left behind a leaner, more-efficient lighthouse system.

Light Construction on the Great Lakes During the Putnam Years

By the time George Putnam rose to power in 1910, the construction of new lighthouses on the Great Lakes was largely over. A few new lights were established after 1910 including the Gary Breakwater Light built in Indiana in 1911, the Sand Hills Light built in Michigan in 1919, Wisconsin's Milwaukee Breakwater Light built in 1926, and the Conneaut West Breakwater Light built in Ohio in 1936. But most other lighthouses built after 1910 were reconstructions or relocations of long-established light stations, or, more rarely, offshore lighthouses built to replace lightships.

Changing configurations in Great Lakes harbors, including the addition of new piers and breakwaters, prompted most of the lighthouse reconstructions or relocations during the Putnam years. For example, Ohio's Fairport Harbor West Breakwater Light was built in 1925 to replace the Old Fairport Main (Grand River) Light on the other side of the river. Michigan's Ludington North Pierhead Light built in 1924 also replaced an earlier harbor light. Ohio's Ashtabula Light, established in 1836 and rebuilt in 1905, was picked up and moved to a newly built, detached breakwater in 1916. The Chicago Harbor Light, established in 1832 and rebuilt for the last time in 1893, was moved in 1917 to a newly built breakwater out in the harbor, where it still stands today.

There were only a few lightships in place on the Great Lakes when George Putnam took over the Bureau of Lighthouses. Putnam fought hard to do away with the lightships and replace them with more-economical lighthouses. During Putnam's tenure, the Bureau of Lighthouses built numerous offshore lighthouses to replace lightships, including the Lansing Shoal Light (1928) in northern Lake Michigan, the Poe Reef Light (1929) in northern Lake Huron, and the North Manitou Shoal Light (1935) in Lake Michigan. By 1940, only the *Lightship Huron* remained in service on the lakes.

The Coast Guard Steps In

On August 7, 1939, President Franklin D. Roosevelt issued an order to dissolve the Bureau of Lighthouses.

Lighthouse administration then fell into the hands of the Coast Guard. The move, an effort to improve efficiency in the government's maritime services by eliminating duplication, was a complete surprise to employees of the Bureau, including H. D. King, Putnam's successor. Under the Coast Guard, Bureau of Lighthouses employees, including all the keepers on the Great Lakes, had the option of joining the Coast Guard or retaining their civilian statuses. Regardless of their decision, they would remain on the job and receive the same salary they were getting before the change. The Great Lakes, in their entirety, became the Ninth Coast Guard District.

The Coast Guard embarked on a general upgrade of lighthouses after World War II replacing many stations that had deteriorated over the years, deactivating many that were no longer needed, and speeding up the process of automating American lighthouses. On the Great Lakes, the Coast Guard rebuilt deteriorating lighthouses such as Michigan's Charlevoix South Pierhead Light and Detroit River Light. The Coast Guard chose to deactivate many more including New York's Braddock Point Light in 1954, Michigan's Old Mackinac Point Light in 1957, and the St. Lawrence River's Rock Island Light in 1958. In the 1950s, 1960s, and 1970s, numerous others would turn off their lights.

Very few Great Lakes lighthouses were automated when the Coast Guard first took over, but by the 1960s, only about eighty lighthouses on the lakes remained manned. In 1983, Wisconsin's Sherwood Point Light became the last American lighthouse on the Great Lakes to be automated, although Coast Guard personnel on leave subsequently used the keeper's house. Canadian lights underwent a similar process. The last Great Lakes lighthouse with a keeper, Battle Island Light in far northern Lake Superior, became automated in 1991. Over a span of fifty years, an entire way of life—that of the lighthouse keeper—had completely vanished from the Great Lakes.

Years of Decline

After considering they stood, in some cases for more than a century, complete with an annual fresh coat of paint, a nicely trimmed lawn, and a flag flapping from a pole in the yard, it is easy to understand why the current state of many Great Lakes lighthouses is truly sad. With the spread of automation, many active lighthouses on the Great Lakes were all but abandoned, visited once a month during the shipping season by a lighthouse

The Bureau of Lighthouses deactivated the Old Fairport Main (Grand River) Light in 1925 after the government activated the Fairport Harbor West Breakwater Light.

tender ship for refueling and maintenance purposes only. No one maintained the grounds or whitewashed the towers and dwellings. The dwellings themselves were boarded up and left to the elements. Sometimes all buildings except the tower itself were torn down.

Active lighthouses that have suffered this fate dot the Great Lakes, particularly in the more remote locations on the upper lakes but also on Lakes Erie and Ontario. The Skillagalee (Ile Aux Galets) Light on northern Lake Michigan lost all of its outbuildings when the station was automated in 1969, and today the active tower stands on its tiny isle alone, with peeling paint and exposed brick. The art deco Indiana Harbor East Breakwater Light never had a keeper; it was automated right from its activation in 1935. This southern Lake Michigan lighthouse is isolated on a long industrial breakwater and looks as if it has been ignored for far longer than its sixty-seven years of existence. But despite the station's broken-down look, it remains active, and some might argue it fits in well with its industrial surroundings. The

lighthouse that stands on tiny Galloo Island in Lake Ontario fifteen miles west of Sackets Harbor was the first American light built on the lake; constructed in 1820, the boarded-up lighthouse certainly looks its age. The paint on the brick has long-since faded, leaving the building with a sandblasted look. The solar panels and antennae around the lantern room are the only clue that this roughed-up station still lights up every evening to guide mariners.

These lighthouses still function, of course. Besides, a lighthouse's purpose is to guide mariners, not to look pretty. It is the deactivated lighthouses on the Great Lakes that really tug at the heartstrings, however. The list of deactivated lights, with problems ranging from loose shingles to the threat of imminent collapse, is long. The lighthouses far from towns or tourist areas have suffered the most.

Although it is abandoned, overgrown, and rundown, the 1892 Squaw Island Light, forty-two miles west of the Mackinac Bridge in northern Lake Michigan, is lucky:

The Bureau of Lighthouses prefabricated the Fairport Harbor West Breakwater Light at the Buffalo Lighthouse Depot then shipped the structure in pieces to Fairport Harbor, Ohio, where it was reassembled. Today, the Fairport Harbor West Breakwater Light remains active on its breakwater stretching out from Headlands Beach State Park.

Its remote location on a privately owned island has largely spared it from vandalism. The station, consisting of a haunted-looking red-brick keeper's house and attached octagonal tower, has the aura of a fixer-upper from a turn-of-the-century neighborhood, and with luck, someone will eventually restore this once-handsome building.

The Turtle Island Light in Lake Erie, four and one-half miles northeast of Toledo, has not been nearly as lucky. The station, established in 1832 and rebuilt in 1866, has been battered by fierce storms throughout its history. Erosion of its tiny island was a constant concern. In 1884, the Lighthouse Board built a retaining wall completely around the perimeter of the island to try to protect the station. But when the shipping channel into Toledo shifted twenty years later, the board deactivated the station and replaced it with the new Toledo Harbor Light. Vandals soon gutted the inactive station. In the 1930s, a yacht club refurbished the Turtle Island Light and used it as their clubhouse for a few years. The

real indignity came in 1965 when a tornado struck Turtle Island, ripping the lantern room from the old tower. Today, only the lanternless, scarred tower remains.

There are a few lighthouses on the lakes that are almost totally destroyed, including Minnesota Point Light in Duluth. Deactivated in 1913, Minnesota Point Light now overlooks a meadow well back from Lake Superior. Only two-thirds of the ragged, empty brick tower remain. In Buffalo Harbor, the Horseshoe Reef Light, deactivated in 1920, is just a rusty skeleton, home to gulls that like to perch on its numerous crossbeams.

One of the most depressing stations on all of the Great Lakes stands at Fourteen Mile Point in Michigan on Lake Superior. Deactivated in 1945, the remote station in the Copper Country State Forest held up fairly well for forty years. But in 1984, a fire set by vandals completely destroyed the interior of the building and the tower, leaving only the brick walls. The fire was so intense that the metal roof of the structure melted away.

Perhaps the most bizarre mishap that led to the virtual destruction of a Great Lakes lighthouse happened during World War II at Waugoshance Light in northern Lake Michigan. The station, deactivated in 1912, was badly damaged when Allied pilots accidentally bombed the lighthouse while practicing on a nearby range. The resulting fire destroyed the interior of the tower and the keeper's quarters. Today, only the tower stands on its fire-scarred crib.

Erosion is another threat to Great Lakes lights. Beachfront stations, particularly remote, deactivated stations, such as Michigan's Crisp Point Light on Lake Superior, are the most threatened. Located about fourteen miles west of the Whitefish Point Light, Crisp Point Light, which was deactivated in 1930, stands on a beach at the end of a two-track road through the Lake Superior State Forest. In 1996, a powerful winter storm destroyed the adjacent fog signal building, and by the summer of 1997, waves were washing nearly to the base of the tower; the resulting erosion threatened to topple the structure. For a time that year, Crisp Point Light was considered the most endangered lighthouse in America and was prominently featured on *Lighthouse Digest*'s Doomsday List of lighthouses in need of immediate attention. The Crisp Point Lighthouse Historical Society raised enough funds to shore up the lighthouse with a stone breakwall in 1998, but the wall only buys some time. Fundraising efforts to save the Crisp Point Light for the long-term continue.

Restoring the Lights

Today, there are many organizations, businesses, and individuals working to save Great Lakes lighthouses, ranging from Dow Chemical to the Boy Scouts. Over the past thirty years or so, people have gathered together to restore many active and inactive lighthouses, often with an eye toward historical accuracy and preservation.

The still-active Big Sable Point Light in Michigan's Ludington State Park is one such success story. Built in 1867, the station was automated and all but abandoned in 1968. But in 1983, the government listed the tower and large keeper's house on the National Register of Historic Places. In 1987, area residents formed the Big Sable Point Lighthouse Keepers Association to restore the lighthouse, which had fallen into disrepair over the years. Since then, association volunteers have restored much of the station, stripping the floors to expose the original red pine woodwork, repairing stairwells and trim around doorways, painting the keeper's house, and more. Their work continues, and the station, with a small

Michigan's Old Mackinac Point Light, established in 1892, marked the turning point for ships passing through the Straits of Mackinac. When the four-mile-long Mackinac Bridge opened in 1957, finally linking the Upper and Lower Peninsulas of Michigan, the Coast Guard deactivated the Old Mackinac Point Light. The lights on the bridge now serve as the aid to navigation.

museum and gift shop staffed by volunteers, is now open to the public. A modest donation buys you the right to climb the 112-foot tower for a stunning view of the rolling sand dunes and Lake Michigan. All proceeds fund the organization's restoration work.

The Grand Island East Channel (South) Light on Lake Superior is also being restored. The goal is not to restore the station to its original condition but to stabilize the 1870 lighthouse and preserve its rustic state. The Lighthouse Board deactivated the well-weathered wooden lighthouse in 1913. As recently as 1999, erosion and structural deterioration threatened to topple the light. Today, the Grand Island East Channel Rescue

A Lighthouse Reborn

The Sand Point Light at Escanaba, Michigan, was built after the Civil War during the Great Lakes lighthouse construction boom. The station's schoolhouse design, consisting of a square tower attached to the front of a two-story keeper's house, was repeated at many Great Lakes lighthouses of the period, from the Granite Island Light on Lake Superior to the Little Traverse Light on Lake Michigan. But the tidy station standing in Escanaba's Ludington Park underwent several transformations to emerge as the lovingly restored, historically accurate lighthouse it is today.

Keeper Mary Terry first lit the Sand Point Light on May 13, 1868. Keeper Terry had assumed her post after the death of her husband John, the appointed keeper who passed away before the lighthouse was activated. The forty-eight-foot tower that marked the entrance to Escanaba Harbor and warned of the sand reef that extended from the point featured a fourth-order Fresnel lens and fixed red light.

In the early morning hours of March 5, 1886, a fire broke out at the lighthouse, badly damaging the interior of the station. As investigators sifted through the ashes, they found the remains of Keeper Mary Terry in the oilroom. The coroner ruled that Terry's death was accidental, but there was some evidence of a break-in and speculation that the keeper was a victim of foul play.

After the tragedy, the Lighthouse Board rebuilt the station. The exterior walls, the foundation, and some of the interior structure survived the fire intact, and builders constructed the new lighthouse dwelling within the walls of the original structure. The Board refurnished and resupplied the station, and the lighthouse was back in operation by late 1886.

By 1938, the harbor at Escanaba had changed so dramatically that the Sand Point Light was no longer effective. That year, construction crews built a new crib lighthouse offshore called the Escanaba Light. In 1939, the Sand Point Light was deactivated.

The Coast Guard used the keeper's dwelling at Sand Point Light to house personnel. Adapting the Sand Point station to its new role, the Coast Guard removed the Fresnel lens and lantern room; knocked ten feet off the top of the tower; raised the roof on the dwelling four feet to accommodate several more rooms on the second floor; removed the circular stairway in the tower and replaced it with a wooden stairway to access the second floor; and cut new windows in the walls to better light the enlarged second floor. Later, the whole structure was sealed in suburban-like aluminum siding. When all was said and done, the Sand Point Light looked like your average boxy house with an odd addition on one side.

And so it remained until 1985, when the Coast Guard decided it no longer needed the residence for personnel. Sensing a unique opportunity to restore a historic structure, the Delta County Historical Society negotiated with the Coast Guard for purchase of the old lighthouse. They reached an agreement, and the historical society immediately went to work raising funds for what would prove to be a mammoth and costly affair—with lovely results.

Aided by the original architectural drawings for the 1867 lighthouse, work commenced in the summer of 1987. Crews removed the aluminum siding and the interior walls on the second floor. They then lowered the roof back to its original height and reproduced the original layout of the second floor.

In the summer of 1988, construction workers laid brick over the windows that had been cut after deactivation, restored the tower to its original height, and replaced the circular iron stairway in the tower. In the summer of 1989, a renewed fundraising effort and extensive volunteer help allowed the historical society to return a lantern room to the tower, using the lantern room from the nearby Poverty Island Light. The workers put in place a fourth-order Fresnel lens that the historical society had had on display at its museum. On December 1, 1989, after sixty years of darkness, the Sand Point Light was relit as a private aid to navigation.

Officially dedicated the following summer, the Sand Point Light opened to the public as a museum. The years had not been kind to the Sand Point Light, but today, the ghost of Keeper Mary Terry can once again stand watch in the lantern room and smile.

The Vermilion Light on Lake Erie in Vermilion, Ohio, dates only from 1991—the lighthouse is a replica of a tower that stood here from 1877 until 1929. Donations from townspeople, businesses, and institutions totaling $62,000 funded the construction of the replica.

When the Coast Guard deactivated the Mendota (Bete Grise) Light in 1960, they removed the station's fourth-order Fresnel lens. The lens resurfaced some thirty-five years later, and the then-owner of the lighthouse had it restored and put back in place in the Mendota lantern room.

Committee works to shore up the erosion and to strengthen the building.

The Vermilion Light in Vermilion, Ohio, on Lake Erie looks much like the 1877 lighthouse that once stood here, but the little lighthouse with its Fresnel lens dates from 1991. The restoration job at Vermilion included the complete reconstruction of the town's lighthouse from scratch. Vermilion's first lighthouse was built as early as 1847, and the lighthouse was rebuilt twice. By 1929, the tower was in danger of collapsing, and the Bureau of Lighthouses sent a tender ship from Buffalo to Vermilion to load up the whole lighthouse and haul it back to Buffalo for repairs. From there, the residents of Vermilion lost track of it. Unknown to the town, the tower was repaired, but instead of being returned to its home in Vermilion, the Bureau transferred it to eastern Lake Ontario, placed it on a crib, and named it the East Charity Shoal Light.

As the years went by, most people forgot about the lighthouse that had vanished. But in the 1980s, Ted Wakefield, a man who grew up in Vermilion and remembered the lighthouse from his childhood, spearheaded a campaign to raise funds to build a historically accurate replica of the old lighthouse. In 1991, sixty-two years after its disappearance, the Vermilion Light was relit.

A few years later, a researcher investigating an entirely different matter stumbled across Bureau of Lighthouses records that described the transfer of the Vermilion Light to East Charity Shoal. The town of Vermilion finally knew what had happened to their historic lighthouse.

In the case of the Mendota (Bete Grise) Light on Lake Superior, the lighthouse's long-missing fourth-order Fresnel lens is at the center of a remarkable restoration story. When the Coast Guard deactivated the station in 1960, the government removed the 1895 lens from the lantern room. From there it vanished.

In the mid 1990s, the then-owner of the Mendota Light Gary Kohs decided to search for the missing lens.

Nine keepers served at the Presque Isle Light near Erie, Pennsylvania, from its establishment in 1873 until its automation in 1944. A road to the lighthouse was not built until 1927. Today, the Presque Isle Light in Presque Isle State Park is home to park employees, though the beacon remains active.

With the help of the Great Lakes Shipwreck Museum at the Whitefish Point Light, he was able to track down the lens in the basement of a Sault Ste. Marie residence. The lens was badly damaged after years of improper handling and storage, so Kohs searched for someone to restore the Fresnel lens. Before long, he stumbled across Robert and Kim Zielinski of Emerald Art Glass in Pittsburgh, Pennsylvania. The Zielinski's business features century-old glass-cutting and grinding equipment, machinery much the same as what would have been used in Paris to create the original lens in the 1890s. With their machinery and some highly detailed refining by hand, the Zielinski's were able to restore the historic lens. Kohs hauled the restored lens back to the lighthouse's lantern room, and on July 5, 1998, the Mendota Light shined again for the first time in thirty-eight years.

Protected Lights

The Great Lakes feature more lighthouses in protected areas—national parks, forests, lakeshores, and state parks and forests—than any other region in the country. From the lighthouses of the Apostle Islands National Lakeshore on Lake Superior to Rock Island Light in the Thousand Islands State Park and Recreation Region on the St. Lawrence River, some fifty lighthouses on the Great Lakes find themselves under government protection within a natural area. Many of these lighthouses have been restored and are open to the public.

Isle Royale National Park on Lake Superior harbors four lighthouses: Passage Island Light, Rock Harbor Light, Menagerie Island (Isle Royale) Light, and Rock of Ages Light. Of these lights, only the Rock Harbor Light is no longer active. The Lighthouse Board deactivated the station in 1879 after activating the Menagerie Island (Isle Royale) Light. Ferries from Grand Portage, Minnesota, to the island pass several of the lighthouses. Visitors can also take water taxis to some of the stations. The gigantic 130-foot tall Rock of Ages Light, built in 1910 off the western end of Isle Royale, is one of the most spectacular offshore lighthouses on the lakes.

Down lake from Isle Royale on the Wisconsin side of Lake Superior, the Apostle Islands National Lakeshore harbors no less than eight lighthouses on its widely scattered islands. Home to the Chequamegon Point Light, La Pointe Light, Michigan Island Old (First) Light and Michigan Island (Second) Light, Raspberry Island Light, Outer Island Light, Devils Island Light, and Sand Island Light, the Apostles have more lighthouses than

any other natural area in the country. Five of the lighthouses still guide ships into Ashland and Bayfield and along the southern shore of Lake Superior. Several of the lighthouses are open to the public. The Apostles are a favorite destination for sailboaters and sea kayakers who sail or paddle from one light station to the next on the sheltered waters between the islands. Lighthouse cruises and water taxis are also available for boatless visitors.

Michigan's Upper Peninsula is the only place in the country where the U.S. Forest Service maintains light stations. The Forest Service controls four lighthouses here: the Round Island (Straits of Mackinac) Light, Point Iroquois Light, Peninsula Point Light, and the Grand Island Harbor Front and Rear Range Lights. Both the Peninsula Point Light and the Point Iroquois Light, which has a museum and gift shop, are open to the public.

Sleeping Bear Dunes National Lakeshore on Lake Michigan has two lighthouses: the North Manitou Shoal Light and the South Manitou Island Light. Ferries travel from Leland, Michigan, to South Manitou Island. The same ferry passes the shoal light and allows access to the island light. The existing South Manitou Island Light, built in 1872, is open to the public during the summer. The whitewashed brick station, like so many lighthouses in protected areas, is in wonderful condition.

On the other side of Michigan on Lake Huron, the Tawas Point Light stands on a stunning peninsula. Protected within Tawas Point State Park, the whitewashed brick tower and red-brick keeper's house remain active—the keeper's house is home to the Coast Guard commander and his family. Wide sandy beaches surround the peninsula, and the park is enormously popular with families during the all-too-brief Michigan summer.

On Lake Erie, the Presque Isle Light and Erie Pierhead Light stand within Presque Isle State Park near Erie, Pennsylvania. The Presque Isle Light, built in 1872 on the Presque Isle Peninsula, is often confused with the Erie Land Light across the bay in Erie, as that lighthouse was originally called the Presque Isle Light. But when the Lighthouse Board built the station on the peninsula, they renamed the light in town the Erie Land Light. Since automation in 1962, the keeper's dwelling at Presque Isle Light has been home to state park employees and Coast Guard personnel. Neither the Presque Isle Light nor the Erie Pier Head Light is open to the public, but both can be viewed up close within the state park.

New York's Thirty Mile Point Light within Golden Hill State Park sits on the edge of a vast campground. The limestone brick lighthouse warns vessels of the shallow sand bar that extends out from the point into Lake Ontario, although the navigational light is now on a nearby skeletal steel tower. Several outbuildings complete the tidy station, and the lighthouse features a museum that is open during the summer. Make reservations early if you plan to camp near the light station, as the campground is generally packed between Memorial Day and Labor Day.

Lighthouse Museums

More than fifty American light stations on the Great Lakes house maritime museums, providing a bonanza of information for the lighthouse buff. Many of these museums/lighthouses allow you climb the tower for a keeper's view of the surrounding waters. The museums display such things as Fresnel lenses, vintage foghorns and bells, keepers' uniforms, compasses and sextants, ship models, and historical photographs.

One of the finest maritime museums on the Great Lakes is the Inland Seas Maritime Museum in Vermilion, Ohio, right next to the Vermilion Light. The expansive museum includes the monumental second-order Fresnel lens from the Spectacle Reef Light on Lake Huron; the fourth-order Fresnel lens (displayed on its turning mechanism) from the Two Harbors Light on Lake Superior; the 450-pound fog bell from the Cleveland West Breakwater Light; scale models of several ships including the *Lightship Huron* and the *Edmund Fitzgerald*; the pilothouse from a lake freighter; and a two-story, complete tugboat engine. For researchers, the neighboring Great Lakes Historical Society library maintains files on nearly every lighthouse on the Great Lakes, with correspondence, historical photographs, newspaper articles, and other items.

The Great Lakes Shipwreck Museum at Michigan's Whitefish Point Light on Lake Superior is another first-class maritime museum. The lighthouse and museum stand along a stretch of coastline known as "The Graveyard of the Great Lakes," where an estimated three hundred ships have sunk throughout history. The museum complex includes the light station's restored keeper's house, which is decorated with period furnishings and open for tours; the active skeletal-steel light tower; and the building that houses the Great Lakes Shipwreck Museum. The station is just seventeen miles southeast

of the final resting place of the *Edmund Fitzgerald*, a taconite freighter that sank with twenty-nine shipmates onboard in a violent 1975 storm. In 1995, the museum, in cooperation with the Canadian Navy, the National Geographic Society, and families of the sailors who died on the *Edmund Fitzgerald*, raised the ship's bell. The bell is on display today at the museum.

Some of the most charming museums are small operations housed in the keeper's quarters of light stations. On Lake Ontario, one of the nicest is the Sodus Bay Lighthouse Museum in Sodus Point, New York, which is operated by the Sodus Bay Historical Society. The displays include a third-and-a-half-order Fresnel lens from Governor's Island Light in New York City, as well as several scale models of ships and of the massive railway coal trestle that once stood at the harbor. The trestle caught fire when it was being dismantled and burned to the ground. The Sodus Point Light is attached to the keeper's house museum, and the tower is open to the public. There's a Fresnel lens in the lantern room. From the top of the tower you can see the nearby Sodus Outer Light, which replaced the Sodus Point Light in 1901, and beautiful Sodus Bay, a natural harbor teeming with islands and sailboats.

Other lighthouses with interesting museums include Lake Michigan's Seul Choix Point Light, Lake Erie's Old Fairport Main (Grand River) Light, Lake Huron's Point Aux Barques Light and Old Presque Isle Light, and Lake Superior's Split Rock Light. There are dozens more, and many other stations across the lakes have informal displays.

The Future of Great Lakes Lighthouses

Built in another era, the lighthouses of the Great Lakes have evolved throughout their history. Technology, from Lewis lamps to Global Positioning Systems, has affected the role of Great Lakes lighthouses, and the lights have changed with the times. Although many lighthouses have fallen into disrepair and some have even been torn down, many more survive, preserved by solid construction and loving caretakers. You can help ensure sunny days ahead for Great Lakes lighthouses. If you visit Great Lakes lighthouses, particularly the ones operated by tiny, underfunded historical societies, make a donation. Preservation costs money. With your help and the efforts of so many others to preserve the lights that remain, the majority of Great Lakes lighthouses can look forward to long and healthy lives along the lakeshore.

The inactive Thirty Mile Point Light in New York's Golden Hill State Park is in marvelous condition today. Several other buildings still stand near the 1876 Lake Ontario tower and keeper's house, including a fog signal building, a round oil house, and a garage/stable.

The original Nine Mile Point Light, built in 1833, still stands on Simcoe Island, Ontario. The lighthouse remains active, guiding ships from Lake Ontario into the St. Lawrence River.

Guide to Great Lakes Lighthouses

Minnesota

Duluth Harbor North Breakwater Light
DULUTH, MINNESOTA
LAKE SUPERIOR

The Duluth Harbor North Breakwater Light, built in 1910, is one of three lights to mark the Lake Superior entrance to the Duluth Ship Canal. At the end of a strollable concrete breakwater, the white, cast-iron, circular tower of the North Breakwater Light tapers upward to support a black lantern room with its active beacon. Although the lighthouse itself is closed to visitors, the Canal Park Marine Museum, at the start of the north breakwater, has exhibits on marine history, including lighthouses.

Duluth Harbor South Breakwater Inner and Outer Lights
DULUTH, MINNESOTA
LAKE SUPERIOR

Along with the Duluth Harbor North Breakwater Light, the South Breakwater Inner (established in 1889) and Outer (established in 1874) Lights help mark the Lake Superior entrance to the Duluth Ship Canal. The existing outer light was built in 1901 and sits at the end of a concrete breakwater on the other side of the canal from the North Breakwater Light. The cylindrical tower is integrated into the red roof of a white, two-story keeper's house. Though you can't enter the lighthouse, you can walk out to it on the pier. The skeletal inner light is also readily accessible next to Duluth's famous Aerial Lift Bridge at the base of the south breakwater.

Grand Marais Light
GRAND MARAIS, MINNESOTA
LAKE SUPERIOR

The present light station at Grand Marais, built in 1922 to replace the original lighthouse established in 1885, sits at the end of the east breakwater at Grand Marais Harbor. The lighthouse has a skeletal base that supports a red-capped watchroom and lantern room. The 1922 lighthouse did not have a keeper's house located on the light station grounds; the original keeper's house was built in downtown Grand Marais and still stands. Now home to a maritime museum operated by the Cook County Historical Society, the original keeper's house is open for tours.

Minnesota Point Light
DULUTH, MINNESOTA
LAKE SUPERIOR

Today, the ruins of the Minnesota Point Light, which was established in 1856 and deactivated in 1913, stand well back from Lake Superior and the Superior Entry waterway. Over time, the lake's waterline has shifted, leaving the light to watch over a grassy clearing. The crumbling red-brick tower has only a ragged top. Its lantern room is long gone.

Split Rock Light
SPLIT ROCK LIGHTHOUSE STATE PARK, MINNESOTA
LAKE SUPERIOR

The Split Rock Light, built in 1910, is one of the most visited lighthouses in the United States. Although the tower is only fifty-four feet tall, it sits atop a 130-foot cliff. Climb the tower to the lantern room for a panoramic view of mighty Lake Superior. While at the top, you can't miss the substantial third-order bivalve Fresnel lens, which rests upon the original, operational mercury-float clockwork turning mechanism. Split Rock Light was deactivated in 1969.

Two Harbors East Breakwater Light
TWO HARBORS, MINNESOTA
LAKE SUPERIOR

The twenty-five-foot-tall Two Harbors East Breakwater Light, established in 1897, rises from the end of a long, angled, concrete pier that extends from shore near the Two Harbors Light. The skeletal base of the small tower supports a watchroom and lantern room with a modern beacon. Visitors can walk along the breakwater to the light, but the lighthouse itself is closed to the public.

Two Harbors Light
TWO HARBORS, MINNESOTA
LAKE SUPERIOR

The still-active Two Harbors Light, established in 1892, is part of a museum complex operated by the Lake County Historical Society. The keeper's house is also a bed-and-breakfast. The square, red-brick tower rises from one corner of the keeper's house to support a white lantern room with a modern beacon. A fog signal building in front of the light includes museum displays and the pilothouse of the freighter *Frontenac*.

Wisconsin

Algoma North Pierhead Light
ALGOMA, WISCONSIN
LAKE MICHIGAN

The Algoma North Pierhead Light, established in 1893, was rebuilt in 1908 and again in 1932, when the harbor was overhauled. Similar to lighthouses along Michigan's western coast, the red lighthouse is attached to a catwalk running along its detached breakwater. Visitors can view the lighthouse from the shore or from the nearby south pier.

Ashland Breakwater Light
ASHLAND, WISCONSIN
LAKE SUPERIOR

The Ashland Breakwater Light, established in 1915, stands at the end of a mile-and-a-half-long rocky, detached breakwater that stretches out from the city of Ashland into Chequamegon Bay. The fifty-eight-foot-tall Ashland Breakwater Light guides vessels into the city's harbor, and landbound visitors can view the light from Ashland's Bayview Park.

Baileys Harbor Front and Rear Range Lights
BAILEYS HARBOR, WISCONSIN
LAKE MICHIGAN

Ship captains complained about the location of the Old Baileys Harbor Light, so this set of range lights was established in 1870 to replace the old station. Today, the inactive lights are part of the Ridges Sanctuary, a natural preserve.

Cana Island Light
NEAR BAILEYS HARBOR, WISCONSIN
LAKE MICHIGAN

Cana Island, located at the end of a peninsula northeast of Baileys Harbor, is attached to the mainland by a causeway that's often submerged. The Door County Maritime Museum maintains the brick keeper's house as well as the steel-plated tower, which was established in 1870. Cana Island Light is one of the most scenic lights on the lakes. A museum and gift shop are inside the keeper's house. The active light tower is not open to the public.

Chambers Island Light
CHAMBERS ISLAND, WISCONSIN
LAKE MICHIGAN

Chambers Island Light, established in 1868 in the middle of Green Bay, has no lantern room. When the lighthouse was deactivated in 1961, lighthouse officials removed the lantern room and Fresnel lens and shipped them to a museum in Minden, Nebraska. Today, the lighthouse is part of a Town of Gibraltar Park.

Chequamegon Point Light
LONG ISLAND, WISCONSIN
LAKE SUPERIOR

Located within the Apostle Islands National Lakeshore on the western edge of Long Island, the existing Chequamegon Point Light was first lit in 1897 to replace an earlier lighthouse that had been established on the site in 1868. The old, skeletal-legged, squat, boxy beacon was deactivated in 1986 when a modern light replaced it. A Coast Guard helicopter lifted up the original lighthouse and moved it back 150 feet from the eroding shoreline.

Devils Island Light
DEVILS ISLAND, WISCONSIN
LAKE SUPERIOR

The original Devils Island Light in the Apostle Islands, established in 1891, was a temporary wooden light. In 1898, construction crews completed an iron light to replace the wooden light. However, three years after the iron light's completion, the wooden light remained active as the lighthouse keeper waited for the the new tower's third-order Fresnel lens to arrive. The Fresnel lens finally arrived, and it remains in the lantern room — Devils Island Light is the only station in the Apostles that still has a Fresnel lens. A modern beacon on the railing outside guides ships through this area today.

Eagle Bluff Light
PENINSULA STATE PARK, WISCONSIN
LAKE MICHIGAN

The Eagle Bluff Light, established deep within Peninsula State Park in 1868, still guides ships through the Strawberry Channel on Green Bay. The Door County Historical Society has restored the station and operates a museum and gift shop in the keeper's house. Climb the fifty-five steps to the lantern room for a closeup look at the fifth-order Fresnel lens and a spectacular view of the bay.

Grassy Island Range Lights
GREEN BAY, WISCONSIN
LAKE MICHIGAN

Since 1872, these lights marked a channel that cut through Grassy Island just north of the city of Green Bay. But in 1966, the Grassy Island Range Lights were deactivated and moved to their present location along the Fox River on the grounds of the Green Bay Yacht Club.

Green Bay Harbor Entrance Light
NEAR GREEN BAY, WISCONSIN
LAKE MICHIGAN

Similar in design to the Peshtigo Reef Light which was built in 1934 a few miles to the north, the Green Bay Harbor Entrance Light marks the main shipping channel into the city of Green Bay. The light, established in 1935, stands nine miles north of the city on a concrete crib.

Green Island Light
NEAR MARINETTE, WISCONSIN
LAKE MICHIGAN

The Green Island Light, established in 1863, is located on its namesake island five miles southeast of Marinette in Green Bay. The light was deactivated in the 1950s when a beacon on a skeletal tower replaced it. The light is now in ruins.

Kenosha North Pier Light
KENOSHA, WISCONSIN
LAKE MICHIGAN

In 1906, the existing tomato-red Kenosha North Pier Light replaced the wooden lighthouse that was built there in 1864. When the new cast-iron pierhead light was lit, the Kenosha (Southport) Light just up the hill was deactivated.

Kenosha (Southport) Light
KENOSHA, WISCONSIN
LAKE MICHIGAN

The fifty-five-foot Kenosha (Southport) Light and nearby keeper's house built of Milwaukee Cream City brick in 1848 still look good today. The light was deactivated in 1906, but in 1994 the light's lantern room, which had been removed in 1913, was replaced with a black metal replica. A new beacon illuminated the tower once again in 1996, though the light does not serve as an official aid to navigation. The Kenosha Historical Society is restoring the station.

Kewaunee Pierhead Light
KEWAUNEE, WISCONSIN
LAKE MICHIGAN

Originally established in 1891 as part of a range light system, the current pierhead light, built in 1931, navigates alone today. The red-capped lantern room houses the active fifth-order Fresnel lens.

La Pointe Light
LONG ISLAND, WISCONSIN
LAKE SUPERIOR

The builders sent to construct the original La Pointe Light mistakenly built it on Michigan Island, well to the northeast of the light's present site in the Apostle Islands. A year later, in 1858, the crew built the La Pointe Light at the intended Long Island location. The existing skeletal tower with a central support column and the nearby red-brick keeper's house went up in 1896.

Longtail Point Light
NEAR GREEN BAY, WISCONSIN
LAKE MICHIGAN

The Longtail Point Light was built of rough limestone on

sandy Longtail Point three miles north of the city of Green Bay in 1848. Just over a decade later, in 1859, the government deactivated the station, fearing the light would collapse, and removed the lantern room. Nearly a century and a half later, the decapitated tower still stands.

Manitowoc North Breakwater Light
MANITOWOC, WISCONSIN
LAKE MICHIGAN

The Manitowoc North Breakwater Light, established in 1895, still uses its fifth-order Fresnel lens to guide vessels into the harbor. Manitowoc is also home to the S.S. Badger car ferry, with regular service across the lake to Ludington, Michigan.

Michigan Island Old (First) Light
MICHIGAN ISLAND, WISCONSIN
LAKE SUPERIOR

After work on this quaint masonry light had been completed in 1857, the contractor discovered he had built the lighthouse on the wrong island—this light should have been built on Long Island. The Lighthouse Service used the light through the 1857 shipping season and then deactivated it. In 1869, Michigan Island Old (First) Light was back in service. It remained active until 1929, when the taller Michigan Island (Second) Light was established nearby. Visitors can see the original third-and-a-half order Fresnel lens from the old light at the Apostle Islands National Lakeshore Visitor's Center in Bayfield.

Michigan Island (Second) Light
MICHIGAN ISLAND, WISCONSIN
LAKE SUPERIOR

The Michigan Island (Second) Light originally stood along the Delaware River near Philadelphia. Crews dismantled the light in 1916 and eventually rebuilt it more than a thousand miles northwest in the Apostle Islands. The light, which stands only one hundred feet from the original much-shorter Michigan Island Old (First) Light, was lit in 1929.

Milwaukee Breakwater Light
MILWAUKEE, WISCONSIN
LAKE MICHIGAN

The Milwaukee Breakwater Light, established in 1926 and automated in 1966, stands at the split in the middle of a nearly four-mile-long breakwater. The square, steel tower of the Milwaukee Breakwater Light rises from a two-story keeper's house.

Milwaukee Pierhead Light
MILWAUKEE, WISCONSIN
LAKE MICHIGAN

Located just south of downtown Milwaukee behind the Summerfest grounds, the red, steel Milwaukee Pierhead Light was built in 1906 to replace a light established in 1872. The Milwaukee Pierhead Light, which is still active, is closed to the public.

North Point Light
MILWAUKEE, WISCONSIN
LAKE MICHIGAN
The North Point Light, established in 1855, is nestled in the Lake Park woods to the north of downtown Milwaukee. The light has a distinctive, octagonal, cast-iron design. Portholes and rectangular windows are staggered like mismatched buttons up several sides of the tower. Workers moved the tower inland to its present location in 1888. In 1913, construction crews nearly doubled the height of the tower to seventy-four feet to make the light visible above the surrounding trees, which had outgrown the previous tower. The light was deactivated in 1994.

Old Baileys Harbor Light
BAILEYS HARBOR, WISCONSIN
LAKE MICHIGAN
From the time it was established in 1852, ship captains thought the Old Baileys Harbor Light was poorly located. When the Baileys Harbor Range Lights took its place in 1870, Old Baileys Harbor Light was deactivated. But the now-privately owned stone tower, located on North Point Island along the eastern side of the harbor, will interest the lighthouse buff. Its birdcage-style lantern room is one of only three of this style remaining on the Great Lakes.

Old Port Washington Light
PORT WASHINGTON, WISCONSIN
LAKE MICHIGAN
The Old Port Washington Light, built in 1860 to replace a station established in 1849, sits on a hill north of downtown Port Washington. The Old Port Washington Light tower, deactivated in 1903, was removed when the nearby breakwater light was rebuilt in 1935. The 1860 keeper's house still stands and is open to the public courtesy of the Port Washington Historical Society. In the spring of 2002, Luxembourger artisans rebuilt the tower and lantern room and returned the replica to the roof of the keeper's house.

Outer Island Light
OUTER ISLAND, WISCONSIN
LAKE SUPERIOR
Appropriately named, Outer Island is the northernmost Apostle Island, the first line of defense against Lake Superior's fury. The original tower and keeper's house, established in 1874, still stand despite more than a century of Mother Nature's wrath. The beacon remains active.

Peshtigo Reef Light
NEAR MARINETTE, WISCONSIN
LAKE MICHIGAN
Shallow, rocky Peshtigo Reef extends three miles into Green Bay from Peshtigo Point, located south of Marinette. Not surprisingly, many ships ran aground on the shoal over the years. More surprisingly, the reef wasn't marked until 1906, when *Lightship No. 77*, also known as the *Peshtigo Reef Lightship*, was put on station. In 1934, an automated tower on a concrete crib replaced the lightship.

Pilot Island (Porte des Morts Passage) Light
PILOT ISLAND, WISCONSIN
LAKE MICHIGAN
The Pilot Island Light today sits remote and lonely on a barren island off the northeastern tip of Door County. In 1858, the original station replaced the nearby Plum Island Light; in fact, the original lighting equipment from the Plum Island Light was removed and installed here. The current station dates from 1873.

Plum Island Front and Rear Range Lights
PLUM ISLAND, WISCONSIN
LAKE MICHIGAN
The range lights on Plum Island help ships navigate the treacherous Porte des Morts (French for "death's door") Passage. Established in 1897, the Front Range Light was rebuilt as a skeletal steel tower in 1964. You can get a good look at the Plum Island Range Lights from the ferry between Northport and Washington Island.

Plum Island (Porte des Morts Passage) Light
PLUM ISLAND, WISCONSIN
LAKE MICHIGAN
The original Plum Island Light, established in 1848, was the second lighthouse built in Door County, but it didn't last long. The government deactivated the shoddily built lighthouse in 1858 and erected a new station on nearby Pilot Island. After the Plum Island light was deactivated, workers moved the station's lighting equipment to the new Pilot Island Light. Today, the long-forgotten station is in ruins.

Port Washington Breakwater Light
PORT WASHINGTON, WISCONSIN
LAKE MICHIGAN
In 1935, the existing art deco Port Washington Breakwater Light replaced the pierhead light that had been established here in 1889.

Potawatomi Light
ROCK ISLAND STATE PARK, WISCONSIN
LAKE MICHIGAN
The Potawatomi Light, located within Rock Island State

Park off the northeastern tip of Washington Island, is the oldest in Wisconsin. Workers completed the light in 1837, and it was lit for the first time the following year. In 1946, after the lighthouse was automated, the Coast Guard unceremoniously removed the light's lantern room. In 1989, crews moved the navigational beacon to a nearby skeletal steel tower. In 1999, as part of an ongoing restoration project, volunteers installed a replica of the old lantern room.

Racine North Breakwater Light
RACINE, WISCONSIN
LAKE MICHIGAN
Locals refer to the Racine North Breakwater Light, established in 1839, as "Big Red." The current tower, which stands near Reefpoint Marina in downtown Racine, was built in 1912. Big Red has held up quite nicely in the intervening ninety or so years. In the 1980s, when the Coast Guard wanted to tear Big Red down, public outcry preserved the landmark.

Raspberry Island Light
RASPBERRY ISLAND, WISCONSIN
LAKE SUPERIOR
The Raspberry Island Light, established in 1863, sits within the Apostle Islands National Lakeshore on a beautiful island forested by old-growth trees—the government-owned island was protected from logging interests. The old lighthouse was deactivated in 1957 when the beacon was moved to a nearby steel pole. During the summer, the station and the light tower are open to the public.

Rawley Point (Twin River Point) Light
NEAR TWO RIVERS, WISCONSIN
LAKE MICHIGAN
Rawley Point's first lighthouse was built in 1854; the currently standing lighthouse was built in Chicago for the 1893 World's Fair and was moved to Rawley Point the following year. The stairway to the lantern room climbs through a very narrow, vertical cylinder, and the entire structure is supported by an octagonal skeletal framework. The active station stands north of Two Rivers, within Point Beach State Forest.

Sand Island Light
SAND ISLAND, WISCONSIN
LAKE SUPERIOR
This active light within the Apostle Islands National Lakeshore stands on the westernmost island in the chain. The original brownstone station, established in 1881, was deactivated in 1933 when a steel beacon tower was built nearby. In 1980, the spiritless modern tower was torn down and the original lighthouse was reactivated. The lighthouse is open for tours during the summer.

Sheboygan Breakwater Light
SHEBOYGAN, WISCONSIN
LAKE MICHIGAN
The earliest lighthouse in Sheboygan dates to 1839, but the first breakwater light was established thirty-four years later. The current red, conical steel tower no longer supports a lantern room, just a tangle of radio antennae, solar panels, and a modern plastic beacon.

Sherwood Point Light
NEAR STURGEON BAY, WISCONSIN
LAKE MICHIGAN
The active Sherwood Point Light has marked the mouth of Sturgeon Bay since 1883. In 1983, it became the last American lighthouse on the Great Lakes to be automated, although the Coast Guard still uses the keeper's house as summer housing for personnel on leave.

Sturgeon Bay Ship Canal Light
NEAR STURGEON BAY, WISCONSIN
LAKE MICHIGAN
The Sturgeon Bay Ship Canal Light, featuring an unusual, narrow, perfectly vertical tower, was built in 1899. Not surprisingly, the tower shook mightily when the winds blew, and the government added a skeletal support frame in 1903. The keeper's house, part of an active Coast Guard station, stands nearby. A breakwater just to the north of the station stretches out to the Sturgeon Bay Ship Canal North Pierhead Light.

Sturgeon Bay Ship Canal North Pierhead Light
NEAR STURGEON BAY, WISCONSIN
LAKE MICHIGAN
The Sturgeon Bay Ship Canal North Pierhead Light opened in 1882—the same time as the Sturgeon Bay Ship Canal. The light sits at the end of a detached breakwater that stretches out from shore just north of the Sturgeon Bay Ship Canal Light. An elevated catwalk runs along the breakwater, connecting the lighthouse to solid ground.

Two Rivers North Pierhead Light
TWO RIVERS, WISCONSIN
LAKE MICHIGAN
The lighthouse in Two Rivers, established in 1883, once stood on the north pierhead. It was deactivated in 1969. In 1988, workers moved the top fifteen feet of the tower to a wooden platform on the grounds of the Rogers Street Fishing Village museum in Two Rivers. The relocated lighthouse is open to the public.

Wind Point Light
WIND POINT, WISCONSIN
LAKE MICHIGAN
The 108-foot-tall Wind Point Light, established in 1880,

towers over the attached keeper's house and the golfers teeing off at the nearby golf course. Located just north of Racine, the whitewashed brick station with green trim remains active. The keeper's house is now the town hall for the village of Wind Point.

Wisconsin Point (Superior Entry South Breakwater) Light
SUPERIOR, WISCONSIN
LAKE SUPERIOR
The oval-shaped keeper's quarters supports this active light. Wisconsin Point Light, established in 1913, marks the western edge of the Superior Entry waterway into Superior Harbor.

Michigan

Alpena Light
ALPENA, MICHIGAN
LAKE HURON
Locally known as "Sputnik" after the Soviet space satellite, the Alpena Light, with its red watchroom and lantern room, sits on a skeletal steel base and looks as if it is ready to orbit the earth. But the old tower, established in 1875, remains firmly earthbound, guiding ships at the mouth of the Thunder Bay River.

Au Sable Point Light
PICTURED ROCKS NATIONAL LAKESHORE, MICHIGAN
LAKE SUPERIOR
The station, including the white, conical brick tower and attached two-story red-brick keeper's house, was established in 1874 and known as the Big Sable Light until 1910. When the Au Sable Point Light was automated in 1958, workers removed the original third-order Fresnel lens and put it in storage in Cleveland. But in 1996, the lens was returned to its proper home in the tower.

Beaver Island (Beaver Head) Light
BEAVER ISLAND, MICHIGAN
LAKE MICHIGAN
In 1858, the tower that stands at the southern end of Beaver Island replaced the tower that had been established at this site in 1852. The station, which has an attached brick-and-woodframe keeper's house, was deactivated in 1962 and is open to the public during the summer. Ferries run between St. James on Beaver Island and Charlevoix on the Michigan mainland year-round.

Big Bay Point Light
NEAR MARQUETTE, MICHIGAN
LAKE SUPERIOR
The pretty Big Bay Point Light, established in 1896, is located twenty-three miles northwest of Marquette. The light features a two-story red-brick keeper's house and attached square tower with a white lantern room. The station was automated in 1941, and in 1961 the beacon was transferred to a nearby steel tower. Today, the lighthouse is a bed-and-breakfast.

Big Sable Point Light
NEAR LUDINGTON, MICHIGAN
LAKE MICHIGAN
In Ludington State Park, the Big Sable Point Light, established in 1867, is a true jewel of a lighthouse and is definitely worth the mile-and-a-half hike to the station and the 130 steps to the top of the tower. In the large keeper's house, which is attached to the black-and-white tower, the Big Sable Lighthouse Keeper's Association operates a museum and gift shop. The lighthouse's third-order Fresnel lens is on display at White Pine Village, south of Ludington.

Bois Blanc Island Light
BOIS BLANC ISLAND, MICHIGAN
LAKE HURON
Bois Blanc Island sits just southeast of Mackinac Island. The first light to stand at this site was established in 1829. The existing tower, built in 1867, is the third to stand on the peninsula that juts from the island's northeastern edge. The light's square tower of yellow brick rises from the front of the keeper's house. When a pole equipped with a solar-powered light was erected nearby in 1955, the station was deactivated. The lighthouse, now privately owned, is not open to the public.

Charity Island Light
BIG CHARITY ISLAND, MICHIGAN
LAKE HURON
In 1857, The Charity Island Light began to warn vessels of the limestone shoal that surrounds Big Charity Island in Saginaw Bay. Located on the northeastern side of the island, the lighthouse was automated in 1900. It was the first Great Lakes station to operate without a keeper. When the nearby Gravelly Shoal Light was built in 1939, the government deactivated Charity Island Light. The tattered station has been neglected for more than sixty years, and it shows.

Charlevoix South Pierhead Light
CHARLEVOIX, MICHIGAN
LAKE MICHIGAN
The earliest light at Charlevoix, erected in 1885, was moved to the south pier at the mouth of the Pine River in 1914. In 1948, construction crews rebuilt the light, and it remains active today. Pretty, Victorian-era Charlevoix is also the docking point for ferry service to Beaver Island, home of the St. James Harbor and Beaver Island Lights.

Cheboygan Crib Light
CHEBOYGAN, MICHIGAN
LAKE HURON
The Cheboygan Crib Light, established in 1852, was located offshore until it toppled and was deactivated in 1988. A diving team retrieved the light and moved it to the base of a pier at the mouth of the Cheboygan River in Gordon Turner Park, where it stands today.

Cheboygan River Front Range Light
CHEBOYGAN, MICHIGAN
LAKE HURON
The Cheboygan River Front Range Light, established in 1880, sits upriver from the Cheboygan Crib Light behind the Medical Center. The wooden square tower rises from the front of a white keeper's house, with two day markers on the front of the tower.

Copper Harbor Front and Rear Range Lights
COPPER HARBOR, MICHIGAN
LAKE SUPERIOR
The original Copper Harbor Rear Range Light, established in 1869, stands just outside Fort Wilkins State Park along Fanny Hooe Creek. The range light was replaced by a nearby skeletal steel light in 1964 and now houses the manager of the state park. The original Front Range Light was replaced by a skeletal steel light down by the water in 1927 and was subsequently torn down.

Copper Harbor Light
COPPER HARBOR, MICHIGAN
LAKE SUPERIOR
The Copper Harbor Light and the Whitefish Point Light, both established in 1849, were the first lighthouses on Lake Superior. Although the Copper Harbor Light was rebuilt in 1866, the original 1849 stone keeper's house still stands next to the 1866 red-brick tower and attached keeper's house. In 1927, the beacon was moved to a nearby steel tower. Today, Fort Wilkins State Park maintains the light station and operates a maritime museum in the 1866 keeper's house.

Crisp Point Light
NEAR TWO HEART, MICHIGAN
LAKE SUPERIOR
The Crisp Point lighthouse, established in 1904, stands alone on a remote beach located fourteen miles west of Whitefish Point. Once the site of a U.S. Life-Saving Service station, a keeper's house, a fog signal building, an oil house, two barns, a boathouse, and more, only the tower and small utility room at its base remain. The lighthouse was deactivated in 1930.

DeTour Reef Light
NEAR DETOUR VILLAGE, MICHIGAN
LAKE HURON
The original 1848 lighthouse stood onshore at DeTour Village, but in 1931, the Bureau of Lighthouses built the current tower on DeTour Reef about a mile offshore. The tower rises from the roof of the keeper's house and is topped by a lantern room with a red cap. In 1974, the station was automated.

Detroit River Light
NEAR GIBRALTAR, MICHIGAN
DETROIT RIVER
A Canadian lightship first marked this area in 1875. In 1885, the Canadian government decommissioned the lightship, which had been anchored about seven miles from Gibraltar at the southern entrance to the Detroit River. The United States Lighthouse Board replaced the lightship with the Detroit River Light. The conical cast-iron tower sits on a concrete crib. The tower was rebuilt in 1951 and automated in 1979.

Eagle Harbor Light
EAGLE HARBOR, MICHIGAN
LAKE SUPERIOR
The red-brick Eagle Harbor Light, established in 1851 and rebuilt twenty years later, remains active in the town of Eagle Harbor on the Keweenaw Peninsula. During the summer, the Keweenaw County Historical Society opens the lighthouse to the public.

Eagle River Light
EAGLE RIVER, MICHIGAN
LAKE SUPERIOR
The existing lighthouse in the town of Eagle River on the Keweenaw Peninsula, built in 1874, replaced the original lighthouse, which was established in 1854. The short tower, deactivated in 1908, rises from the roof of a woodframe house, which is now a private residence. Today, a condominium stands between the lake and the inactive lighthouse, obscuring it from the view of boaters out on the lake.

Escanaba Light
ESCANABA, MICHIGAN
LAKE MICHIGAN
The offshore Escanaba Light, established in 1938, replaced the nearby Sand Point Light. The Coast Guard automated the light in 1976. You can get a good look at this active shoal light from the grounds of the Sand Point Light in Escanaba's Ludington Park.

Fort Gratiot Light
PORT HURON, MICHIGAN
LAKE HURON

The first lighthouse at Fort Gratiot, established in 1825, lasted only four years before it was destroyed in a storm. The 1829 replacement fared better. It still stands in Port Huron, just north of the Bluewater Bridge to Ontario. The Coast Guard lovingly maintains the active station, and the spit-polished white tower with red trim is in immaculate condition.

Forty Mile Point Light
NEAR MANITOU BEACH, MICHIGAN
LAKE HURON

Forty Mile Point Light's square, white-brick tower and attached red-brick keeper's house, established in 1896, stands within Presque Isle County Lighthouse Park. On the beach to the north of the light, the timbers of a shipwreck are buried in the sand.

Fourteen Foot Shoal Light
NEAR CHEBOYGAN, MICHIGAN
LAKE HURON

Established in 1930, the Fourteen Foot Shoal Light can be seen from the beach in Cheboygan State Park. The conical tower that rises from the center of a one-story utility building never has had a keeper; the keepers at the nearby Poe Reef Light operated the lighthouse by radio.

Fourteen Mile Point Light
NEAR ONTONAGON, MICHIGAN
LAKE SUPERIOR

The privately owned Fourteen Mile Point Light, established in 1894, stands within the Copper Country State Forest about fifteen miles east of Ontonagon. The light was deactivated in 1945, and in 1984 a fire set by vandals gutted the once proud station.

Frankfort North Breakwater Light
FRANKFORT, MICHIGAN
LAKE MICHIGAN

Frankfort North Breakwater Light's square, tapered white tower rises above the north breakwater at the mouth of the Betsie River. In 1932, the Bureau of Lighthouses erected the current steel tower to replace the original light, which was established in 1873.

Frying Pan Island Light
SAULT STE. MARIE, MICHIGAN
ST. MARY'S RIVER

This cast-iron light, established in 1887, originally stood on Frying Pan Island, just downriver from DeTour Village. When a modern beacon was erected on the island, workers moved the tower to the Sault Ste. Marie Coast Guard Station.

Grand Haven Lights
GRAND HAVEN, MICHIGAN
LAKE MICHIGAN

An elevated catwalk running along a pier connects the two red lighthouses, at the mouth of the Grand River in Grand Haven, to the shore. The Outer Light, which pokes from the roof of a fog signal building, dates to 1839. Construction crews built the current tower in 1905 when they erected the present pier. That same year, the Lighthouse Board added the Inner Light to the new pier, creating a range system.

Grand Island East Channel (South) Light
GRAND ISLAND, MICHIGAN
LAKE SUPERIOR

Known locally as the South Light, the wooden tower and attached keeper's house on the southeastern shore of Grand Island, established in 1870, looks as if it should be in a western ghost town. The now-dilapidated lighthouse was abandoned in 1913 after the Munising Front and Rear Range Lights were built. Although Grand Island is a National Recreation Area, the lighthouse itself is on private property.

Grand Island Harbor Front and Rear Range Lights
CHRISTMAS, MICHIGAN
LAKE SUPERIOR

Depending on who you ask, these lighthouses are also known as the Christmas Lights and the End of the Road Range Lights. The existing steel Rear Range Light was built in 1914, replacing the original 1868 light. The Front Range Light, added in 1915, was torn down in 1969 and replaced by a directional beacon, which was then replaced by another beacon in 1985. The lighthouses, located within the Hiawatha National Forest, are owned by the U.S. Forest Service.

Grand Island Old North Light
GRAND ISLAND, MICHIGAN
LAKE SUPERIOR

The original Grand Island Old North Light, built in 1855, stood on a 175-foot cliff along the north side of Grand Island. The existing square brick tower and attached keeper's house replaced the original station in 1867. When the Coast Guard placed an automated light on a pole nearby in 1961, the lighthouse was deactivated. The pole beacon remains active. The lighthouse and keeper's house still stand, but they are privately owned, and are not open to the public.

Grand Marais Front and Rear Range Lights
GRAND MARAIS, MICHIGAN
LAKE SUPERIOR

The Front Range Light, established in 1895, and the Rear Range Light, established in 1898, aid vessels searching for the only harbor of refuge between Whitefish Point and Munising. Both towers are skeletal steel with a small, square watchroom just below the lantern. The Grand Marais Historical Society has converted the keeper's house into the Lighthouse Keepers Museum.

Grand Traverse (Cat's Head) Light
LEELANAU STATE PARK, MICHIGAN
LAKE MICHIGAN

Locally known as Cat's Head Light, the existing Grand Traverse Light is located twenty-five miles north of Traverse City within Leelanau State Park. The light, built in 1858, replaced the shoddily built original light, which had been established in 1853. The lighthouse remained active until 1972, when its beacon was moved nearby to a skeletal steel tower. The keeper's house now houses a museum and gift shop.

Granite Island Light
NEAR MARQUETTE, MICHIGAN
LAKE SUPERIOR

First lit in the spring of 1869 on a tiny, rocky isle eleven miles north of Marquette, the Granite Island Light was abandoned when the light was moved to a skeletal steel tower near the station in 1939. The skeletal steel tower light remains active.

Gravelly Shoal Light
NEAR POINT LOOKOUT, MICHIGAN
LAKE HURON

This art deco beacon, built in 1939, replaced the nearby Charity Island Light, which was then deactivated. Never manned, the square tower on a circular concrete base tapers to support a modern beacon and a skeletal steel radio tower. You'll need a boat to get a good view of this light.

Gray's Reef Light
NEAR BEAVER ISLAND, MICHIGAN
LAKE MICHIGAN

A lightship first marked this area in 1891. The existing eight-sided art deco tower, located twenty-four miles west of the Mackinac Bridge, was built in 1936. The whitewashed station, topped with a black lantern room and skeletal steel radio tower, sits on a thickset concrete crib.

Grosse Ile North Channel Front Range Light
GROSSE ILE, MICHIGAN
DETROIT RIVER

Originally part of a range system, the current Grosse Ile North Channel Front Range Light, on the northeastern side of the island near Detroit, was built in 1906 to replace a light built on the site in 1894; the companion Rear Range Light no longer stands. The octagonal, wooden tower of the lighthouse, which stands at the end of a pier, was deactivated in 1963 and is now owned by the Grosse Ile Historical Society.

Gull Rock Light
NEAR MANITOU ISLAND, MICHIGAN
LAKE SUPERIOR

Tiny Gull Rock, located about two miles off the tip of the Keweenaw Peninsula, is barely larger than the brick light tower, attached keeper's house, and adjacent oil house that sit on top of it. Gull Rock Light was established in 1867.

Harbor Beach Light
HARBOR BEACH, MICHIGAN
LAKE HURON

The earliest lighthouse at Harbor Beach was established in 1858, but the current lighthouse was erected in 1885 when the detached breakwater was built in the harbor.

Holland Harbor Light
HOLLAND, MICHIGAN
LAKE MICHIGAN

Known locally as "Big Red," the existing 1936 Holland Harbor Light replaced the original light on this site, which had been established in 1872. The twin-peaked building that supports the tower housed the fog signal equipment. Private property impedes direct access to the light, but you can get a closeup view of the station from Holland State Park, located just across the channel.

Huron Island Light
WEST HURON ISLAND, MICHIGAN
LAKE SUPERIOR

The granite Huron Island Light, established in 1868, stands on a 160-foot cliff on West Huron Island, three miles off-shore and thirty miles northwest of Marquette. The lighthouse was built at the same time as the very similar Granite Island Light. West Huron Island is part of the Huron Islands Wilderness Area, which is part of the Seney National Wildlife Refuge.

Keweenaw Waterway (Portage River) Lower Entrance Light
JACOBSVILLE, MICHIGAN
LAKE SUPERIOR

Located on the east pier at the entrance to the Keweenaw Waterway on Keweenaw Bay, the existing lighthouse dates to 1920. The first lighthouse to stand here was established in 1868. You can walk out to the light on the pier, but on foggy days, beware: The powerful fog signal will send you reeling.

Keweenaw Waterway Upper Entrance Light
NEAR HOUGHTON, MICHIGAN
LAKE SUPERIOR

The earliest lighthouse at the entrance to the Keweenaw Waterway on the Lake Superior side dates to 1874. As breakwaters were built, other lights were established. Construction crews widened the canal in the 1930s and eventually tore down the 1874 light. The current art deco lighthouse, erected in 1950 and never manned, stands on a crib just off the end of a treacherous, knee-shredding breakwall that stretches from shore at F. J. McClain State Park.

Lake St. Clair Light
NEAR ST. CLAIR SHORES, MICHIGAN
LAKE ST. CLAIR
The Lake St. Clair Light, established in 1941, marks a bend in the busy shipping channel that cuts through the middle of the lake. The white octagonal tower with a green stripe sits on a round steel-and-concrete crib.

Lansing Shoal Light
NEAR ST. JAMES, MICHIGAN
LAKE MICHIGAN
From 1900 until 1928, *Lightship No. 55* marked this dangerous shoal nine miles north of Beaver Island; the current lighthouse replaced the lightship in 1928. The square concrete tower rises from the center of a one-story metal building built on top of a broad, square concrete crib. The original third-order Fresnel lens, removed in the 1980s, is on display at the Michigan Historical Museum in Lansing.

Lightship Huron
PORT HURON, MICHIGAN
LAKE HURON
The Bureau of Lighthouses originally stationed the *Lightship Huron* in northern Lake Michigan in 1921, but the Bureau reassigned the ship to the Corsica Shoals off Port Huron in 1935. The *Huron*, the last lightship in service on the Great Lakes, was retired in 1970. The city of Port Huron now operates the lightship as a landlocked museum in Pine Grove Park on the St. Clair River.

Little Sable Point Light
NEAR SHELBY, MICHIGAN
LAKE MICHIGAN
The 107-foot-tall brick Little Sable Point Light, established in 1874, looms over the beach in a remote section of Silver Lake State Park. The tower is all that remains of the station. When the light became automated in 1955, construction crews demolished the once-nearby keeper's house.

Little Traverse (Harbor Point) Light
NEAR HARBOR SPRINGS, MICHIGAN
LAKE MICHIGAN
Elizabeth Whitney Van Riper Williams was the first keeper of the red-brick lighthouse located on Harbor Point on the northern side of Little Traverse Bay. In 1905, she published *A Child of the Sea*, an autobiography of her life on the lakes. Today, the square tower and attached keeper's house, which were established in 1884, sit within a gated community and

are not accessible by land. The skeletal steel light that stands nearby replaced the lighthouse in 1963.

Ludington North Pierhead Light
LUDINGTON, MICHIGAN
LAKE MICHIGAN
Although a light marked this area as early as 1871, the current Ludington North Pierhead Light was built in 1924. The white steel tower, with a black lantern room, sits at the end of a breakwater in Ludington Harbor. For a view of the lighthouse from the harbor, board the S.S. *Badger* car ferry, with regular service to Manitowoc, Wisconsin.

Manistee North Pierhead Light
MANISTEE, MICHIGAN
LAKE MICHIGAN
The existing Manistee North Pierhead Light, built in 1927, replaced the original light built in 1875. A steel catwalk stretches along the breakwater from the Fifth Avenue Beach to the sturdy round steel tower. The catwalk, a feature common to pierhead lights in this part of Michigan, provided safer access to the light in stormy weather.

Manistique East Breakwater Light
MANISTIQUE, MICHIGAN
LAKE MICHIGAN
The cast-iron Manistique East Breakwater Light at the mouth of the Manistique River was established in 1915 and automated in 1969. Although the tower is closed to the public, the porthole-studded, red lighthouse is accessible in good weather by walking along the breakwater.

Manitou Island Light
MANITOU ISLAND, MICHIGAN
LAKE SUPERIOR
In 1850, the government established the first lighthouse on Manitou Island, located a few miles off the tip of the Keweenaw Peninsula. The present lighthouse replaced the original lighthouse in 1861. The eighty-foot tower consists of a central column supported by a skeletal framework. A covered walkway connects the light to a wooden keeper's house.

Marquette Harbor Light
MARQUETTE, MICHIGAN
LAKE SUPERIOR
The primitive wooden lighthouse built at Marquette Harbor in 1853 lasted only thirteen years. The current lighthouse, built in 1866, has proved much sturdier. The red, square tower and attached brick keeper's house sit on a bluff overlooking the harbor. At the end of a breakwater that extends out from the shoreline below the Marquette Harbor Light stands the Marquette Lower Harbor Breakwater Light. When the lighthouses were manned, the keeper of the

Marquette Harbor Light tended both lights. The lower harbor light, established in 1867, was replaced with a modern cylinder beacon when both stations were automated in the 1980s.

Martin Reef Light
NEAR CEDARVILLE, MICHIGAN
LAKE HURON

The many vessels that travel along Michigan's Upper Peninsula between the St. Mary's River and the Straits of Mackinac rely on the Martin Reef Light to mark a treacherous reef about ten miles south of Cedarville. The fat, square, white tower narrows at its red top. The structure, similar in design to the Poe Reef Light fifteen miles to the south, sits on a concrete crib. Martin Reef Light was established in 1927.

McGulpin's Point Light
MACKINAW CITY, MICHIGAN
LAKE MICHIGAN

The McGulpin's Point Light, established about two miles west of Mackinac Point in 1856, was once the main beacon in this area. In 1892, after mariners complained that it was in a poorly chosen location, the Old Mackinac Point Light replaced McGulpin's Point Light. Despite its replacement, McGulpin's Point Light remained active until 1906. Today, the lantern room is gone from the red-trimmed brick structure and the station is a private residence.

Menagerie Island (Isle Royale) Light
ISLE ROYALE NATIONAL PARK, MICHIGAN
LAKE SUPERIOR

The Menagerie Island Light, established in 1875, sits on a tiny, rocky island just south of Isle Royale. Four years after this lighthouse was built, the Rock Harbor Light, fifteen miles east of Menagerie Island, was deactivated.

Mendota (Bete Grise) Light
BETE GRISE, MICHIGAN
LAKE SUPERIOR

The Mendota (Bete Grise) Light, established in 1870, stands near the entrance to the Mendota Ship Canal, which connects Bete Grise Bay and Lac la Belle. The tower contains the restored 1895 fourth-order Fresnel lens. You can get a nice view of the station across the canal in the village of Bete Grise. The lighthouse, which was deactivated in 1960, is privately owned and closed to the public.

Menominee North Pier Light
MENOMINEE, MICHIGAN
LAKE MICHIGAN

The cast-iron Menominee North Pier Light sits at the mouth of the Menominee River. The current red tower was built in 1927, but the original light was established here in 1877.

Middle Island Light
MIDDLE ISLAND, MICHIGAN
LAKE HURON

The Middle Island Light, established in 1905, sits on the eastern side of the island three miles offshore and ten miles north of Alpena. The Middle Island Lighthouse Keeper's Association is currently restoring the light in hopes of turning the handsome, gabled roof keeper's house into a bed-and-breakfast.

Minneapolis Shoal Light
NEAR ESCANABA, MICHIGAN
LAKE MICHIGAN

The Minneapolis Shoal Light, first lit in 1935, is about ten miles south of Escanaba in Green Bay. Shortly after the art deco tower of steel and reinforced concrete was activated, the Bureau of Lighthouses extinguished Peninsula Point Light. The Minneapolis Shoal Light contains a working fourth-order Fresnel lens. If you lack a seaworthy boat but have binoculars, you can see the light from the Peninsula Point Light tower.

Munising Front and Rear Range Lights
MUNISING, MICHIGAN
LAKE SUPERIOR

Both of these range towers, established in 1908, have active, locomotive-style beacons. The towers are white, conical, and built of riveted steel plates. The front range light is fifty-eight feet tall, and the rear range light is shorter, though it sits a considerable distance uphill and therefore has a higher focal plane. The establishment of this range system led to the deactivation of the Grand Island East Channel Light in 1913.

Muskegon South Pierhead Light
MUSKEGON, MICHIGAN
LAKE MICHIGAN

Several signal beacons have marked the piers near the entrance to Muskegon Lake since 1851. The iron, cylindrical South Pierhead Light that presently stands at the end of the pier extending from the Muskegon Coast Guard Station is red from top to bottom.

North Manitou Shoal Light
NEAR LELAND, MICHIGAN
LAKE MICHIGAN

A lightship marked the North Manitou Shoal, located about halfway between Leland and North Manitou Island, from 1910 until the North Manitou Shoal Light was built in 1935. A concrete crib supports the square tower on a larger, two-story square dwelling. To see the lighthouse, take one of the many ferries traveling from Leland to North and South Manitou Islands within Sleeping Bear Dunes National Lakeshore.

Old Cheboygan Light Ruins
NEAR CHEBOYGAN, MICHIGAN
LAKE HURON

The Old Cheboygan Light, established in 1851, was replaced by the Fourteen Foot Shoal Light in 1930. Old Cheboygan Light was abandoned and eventually torn down, leaving only rubble. The stroll to the ruins along the woodsy path in Cheboygan State Park is leisurely; if you walk out to the beach near the ruins, you can get a nice view of both the Fourteen Foot Shoal Light and the Poe Reef Light offshore.

Old Mackinac Point Light
MACKINAW CITY, MICHIGAN
LAKE HURON

Old Mackinac Point Light replaced a fog signal that marked the area from 1890 until 1892. The castle-like structure also replaced the McGulpin's Point Light, which mariners thought to be poorly located. The Old Mackinac Point Light remained active until 1957 when the Mackinac Bridge was built west of the lighthouse. The bridge lights were bright enough to guide vessels through the area. Today, the fog signal building near the lighthouse is home to a gift shop and the grounds are part of Lakeshore Park.

Old Mission Point Light
OLD MISSION, MICHIGAN
LAKE MICHIGAN

The Old Mission Point Light, established in 1870, lies eighteen miles due north of Traverse City; it is at the tip of a narrow peninsula that juts out into Grand Traverse Bay. Old Mission Point Light was deactivated in 1933. The lighthouse building is private property, but the grounds are open to the public.

Old Presque Isle Light
PRESQUE ISLE, MICHIGAN
LAKE HURON

One of four lighthouses around Presque Isle, the Old Presque Isle Light was built in 1840. In 1871, when the new Presque Isle Light was activated about a mile away at the tip of the peninsula, the Old Presque Isle Light went out of service. Today, Old Presque Isle Light, hidden at the end of a winding road through a dense pine forest, serves as a museum.

Ontonagon Light
ONTONAGON, MICHIGAN
LAKE SUPERIOR

The Ontonagon Light, established in 1853, was built away from the lake along the banks of the Ontonagon River; today, the light is surrounded by an industrial complex. Ontonagon Light was deactivated in 1964, and the Ontonagon Historical Society maintains the lighthouse. Inquire at the historical society museum located a few blocks from the river on River Street if you wish to visit the station. The lighthouse's fifth-order Fresnel lens, which dates to 1857, is on display at the museum.

Ontonagon West Pierhead Light
ONTONAGON, MICHIGAN
LAKE SUPERIOR

Established in 1884, Ontonagon West Pierhead Light is perched on top of a twenty-foot-tall skeletal steel tower at the mouth of the Ontonagon River. The light is 1,000 feet from the inactive Ontonagon Light.

Passage Island Light
ISLE ROYALE NATIONAL PARK, MICHIGAN
LAKE SUPERIOR

The fieldstone lighthouse on Passage Island, located off the northeastern tip of Isle Royale, is the most northerly American lighthouse on the Great Lakes. To visit the station, which was established in 1882 and has been automated since 1978, you can take a ferry from Isle Royale directly to Passage Island.

Peche Island Light
MARINE CITY, MICHIGAN
ST. CLAIR RIVER

The Peche Island Light, established in 1908, originally stood on Ontario's Peche Island at the Lake St. Clair entrance to the Detroit River. In 1983, the steel lighthouse was deactivated and moved to its present location in a park along the St. Clair River in Marine City.

Peninsula Point Light
STONINGTON, MICHIGAN
LAKE MICHIGAN

The square brick tower of the Peninsula Point Light, established in 1866, is all that remains of this station, located twenty miles south of Rapid River. After the Peninsula Point Light was deactivated in 1936, the once-attached keeper's house was destroyed by fire. The National Forest Service administers the site, and the tower is open to the public. The now-empty lantern room provides a clear view of the 1935 Minneapolis Shoal Light, which replaced this station.

Pipe Island Light
PIPE ISLAND, MICHIGAN
ST. MARY'S RIVER

This octagonal brick tower, established in 1888, stands at the southern edge of Pipe Island in the lower St. Mary's River. In 1937, construction crews removed the lantern room and built a skeletal steel structure on top of the original tower in order to raise the beacon. The island is privately owned, and there is no public access to this light station.

Poe Reef Light
NEAR CHEBOYGAN, MICHIGAN
LAKE HURON

From 1893 until this lighthouse was built in 1929, a lightship marked Poe Reef. The Cheboygan State Park beach near the Old Cheboygan Light Ruins provides a distant view of this lighthouse and the Fourteen Foot Shoal Light.

Point Betsie Light
NEAR FRANKFORT, MICHIGAN
LAKE MICHIGAN

The Point Betsie Light, established in 1858 and manned until 1983, was one of the last American lights on the Great Lakes to be automated. Today, the white stucco keeper's house and attached white brick tower are maintained by Benzie County and are not open to the public. For a nice view of the station, travel along the access road to the beach. The original fourth-order Fresnel lens, removed in 1996, is on display at the Sleeping Bear Point Life-Saving Maritime Museum in Empire. Although it is privately owned and not open to the public, the Point Betsie Life-Saving Station is just across the road from the lighthouse. Look for the watchtower poking from the roof of the building.

Point Iroquois Light
NEAR BAY MILLS, MICHIGAN
LAKE SUPERIOR

In 1871, the current conical brick tower and attached keeper's house replaced the original lighthouse that had marked Point Iroquois since 1855. The station, located at the entrance to the St. Mary's River on Lake Superior, was automated in 1962. When the Canadian Gros Cap Reef Light was built in 1971, the station was deactivated. The station's fourth-order Fresnel lens was transferred to the Smithsonian Institution in Washington, D.C. The U.S. Forest Service manages the site today, and there is a museum and gift shop in the keeper's house.

Pointe Aux Barques Light
PORT HOPE, MICHIGAN
LAKE HURON

Despite its name, the Pointe Aux Barques Light actually stands fifteen miles southeast of Pointe Aux Barques, near Port Hope. The current Pointe Aux Barques Light was built in 1857 to replace a not-so-sturdy light built in 1848. Today, the active station is also home to a maritime museum. At the nearby Huron City Museum, you can visit the old life-saving station that was originally located near the lighthouse.

Port Austin Reef Light
NEAR PORT AUSTIN, MICHIGAN
LAKE HURON

The sturdy, four-story, brick tower at Port Austin Reef, established in 1878, sits on a broad, octagonal, concrete foundation just off the "thumb" of Michigan's Lower Peninsula. The existing tower and attached keeper's house were rebuilt in 1899, and the station was automated in 1953. The numerous shipwrecks nearby, now part of an underwater park for divers called the Thumb Area Bottomland Preserve, are proof that this area needs a lighthouse.

Port Sanilac Light
PORT SANILAC, MICHIGAN
LAKE HURON

The octagonal, brick Port Sanilac Light tapers toward its top and then flares outward to support the lantern room, complete with a fourth-order Fresnel lens. The attached red-brick keeper's house is a private residence, although the lighthouse, which was established in 1886, remains active.

Portage River (Jacobsville) Light
JACOBSVILLE, MICHIGAN
LAKE SUPERIOR

The Portage River (Jacobsville) Light, was established in 1856 and is located about a half mile up the shore from the Keweenaw Waterway (Portage River) Lower Entrance Light. Portage River (Jacobsville) Light was deactivated in 1900 and is a private residence today. Although dark for more than a century, the old lighthouse is in very good condition.

Poverty Island Light
NEAR ESCANABA, MICHIGAN
LAKE MICHIGAN

The Poverty Island Light station, established at the entrance to Green Bay in 1875, is near ruin. The conical brick tower lacks a lantern room and was deactivated in 1976, but it does support a beacon, which was reactivated in 1982. The skeletal steel light nearby was erected in 1976.

Presque Isle Harbor Front and Rear Range Lights
PRESQUE ISLE, MICHIGAN
LAKE HURON

The Rear Range Light is a schoolhouse-style building along the road to the Old Presque Isle Light and the Presque Isle Light. The petite Front Range Light once stood closer to the old Rear Range Light, but today rests just under a mile away at the beginning of the access road to the Old Presque Isle Light. Both beacons, which were established in 1870, have been replaced by skeletal steel range lights.

Presque Isle Harbor (Marquette) Breakwater Light
MARQUETTE, MICHIGAN
LAKE SUPERIOR

This steel and concrete tower has stood since 1941 at the end of the rocky breakwater that extends from Presque Isle Peninsula north of downtown Marquette.

Presque Isle Light
PRESQUE ISLE, MICHIGAN
LAKE HURON

The imposing "new" Presque Isle Light towers 113 feet above the ground. Built in 1871, the lighthouse replaced the much smaller and not as well positioned Old Presque Isle Light, which stands about a mile away. Although the light station is still active, it also houses a public museum and gift shop. The original third-order Fresnel lens remains in the lantern room.

Robert H. Manning Memorial Light
EMPIRE, MICHIGAN
LAKE MICHIGAN

Though not an official navigational aid, the Robert H. Manning Memorial Light is functional and ably serves the memory of its namesake, an Empire-area fisherman who longed for a light to guide him home after long days of fishing the lake. The fisherman's family built the lighthouse after his death in 1989.

Rock Harbor Light
ISLE ROYALE NATIONAL PARK, MICHIGAN
LAKE SUPERIOR

Rock Harbor Light, built of rough, whitewashed stone in 1855, stands on the southeast side of Isle Royale. The light was deactivated in 1879 and replaced by the Menagerie Island (Isle Royale) Light. In the 1960s, the National Park Service restored Rock Harbor Light which now houses a museum.

Rock of Ages Light
ISLE ROYALE NATIONAL PARK, MICHIGAN
LAKE SUPERIOR

The 130-foot Rock of Ages Light, established off the southwestern tip of Isle Royale in 1908, exhibited a temporary light until a second-order Fresnel lens was installed in 1910. The Fresnel lens is now on display at the Windigo Visitor's Center on Isle Royale.

Round Island Passage Light
NEAR MACKINAC ISLAND, MICHIGAN
LAKE HURON

The Round Island Passage Light, a hexagonal steel and concrete tower, replaced the nearby 1896 Round Island (Straits of Mackinac) Light in 1947. Located just off the south shore of Mackinac Island, the new light stands closer to the shipping channel to better guide vessels sailing the Straits.

Round Island (St. Mary's River) Light
ROUND ISLAND, MICHIGAN
ST. MARY'S RIVER

Located in the Lower St. Mary's River near Lime Island, this wooden light, established in 1892, was eventually replaced by a light on a pole. Today, the Round Island (St. Mary's River) Light is inactive and privately owned.

Round Island (Straits of Mackinac) Light
ROUND ISLAND, MICHIGAN
LAKE HURON

The Round Island (Straits of Mackinac) Light, perched on the northwestern tip of Round Island, just south of Mackinac Island, is one of Michigan's most viewed lighthouses, as it sits along the ferry line from Mackinaw City to the heavily touristed Mackinac Island. The light, established in 1896, was deactivated in 1947 and was severely damaged in a 1972 gale. But the square brick tower and attached keeper's house are undergoing restoration, and in 1996, the station was re-activated as a private aid to navigation.

Saginaw River Rear Range Light
SAGINAW, MICHIGAN
LAKE HURON

The Saginaw River Rear Range Light was built in 1876 to replace the original lighthouse established in 1841. Saginaw River Rear Range Light was deactivated in 1960. Today, using funds from lighthouse owner Dow Chemical, the Saginaw River Marine Historical Society is restoring the lighthouse. Though the lighthouse is not open to the public, it can be seen from the grounds of the Coast Guard station on the opposite side of the river.

Sand Hills Light
NEAR AHMEEK, MICHIGAN
LAKE SUPERIOR

The Sand Hills Light was established on Five Mile Point, eight miles northeast of Ahmeek, in 1919. The light was deactivated in 1954 and is now a bed-and-breakfast. The massive keeper's house was built to house two keepers and their families.

Sand Point (Baraga) Light
BARAGA, MICHIGAN
LAKE SUPERIOR

Located within the L'Anse Indian Reservation, the Sand Point (Baraga) Light, established in 1878, was replaced by a nearby skeletal steel light and is no longer active. The privately owned, red-brick lighthouse has a porch that faces Keweenaw Bay.

Sand Point (Escanaba) Light
ESCANABA, MICHIGAN
LAKE MICHIGAN

In 1886, a fire destroyed the first Sand Point Light, which had been built in 1868, and killed the keeper, Mary Terry. The lighthouse was rebuilt and stayed in service until 1939.

In the 1980s, the Delta County Historical Society restored the lighthouse building and tower. The society reopened the station as a museum in 1990. The building behind the lighthouse also houses a historical society museum.

Seul Choix Point Light
NEAR GULLIVER, MICHIGAN
LAKE MICHIGAN
The Seul Choix Point Light, established in 1895, is one of the prettiest lighthouses on the Great Lakes. The light sits on the southern shore of the Upper Peninsula eight miles south of Gulliver and marks a limestone shoal that extends from the point. The interior of the keeper's house features the original woodwork and period furnishings. Visitors can climb the eighty-foot tower. The original oil house and fog signal building still stand nearby.

Skillagalee (Ile Aux Galets) Light
NEAR WAUGOSHANCE ISLAND, MICHIGAN
LAKE MICHIGAN
The whitewashed, brick Skillagalee Light, established in 1850, sits on tiny Ile Aux Galets located southwest of Waugoshance Island. The current station, built in 1888, is the third on the island. A keeper's house and several outbuildings were torn down in 1969.

South Fox Island Lights
SOUTH FOX ISLAND, MICHIGAN
LAKE MICHIGAN
Both lighthouses on the southern end of South Fox Island, twenty-six miles west of Charlevoix, sit abandoned and inactive today. The original 1868 brick lighthouse and attached keeper's house were replaced in 1934 by a nearby steel tower and keeper's house.

South Haven South Pier Light
SOUTH HAVEN, MICHIGAN
LAKE MICHIGAN
The Lighthouse Board built the current South Haven South Pier Light at the mouth of the Black River in 1903 to replace the light established there in 1872. In 1913, the Bureau of Lighthouses moved the light to its present location at the end of the South Pier. A catwalk runs along the pier to the little red tower. The area around the station is a public park.

South Manitou Island Light
SOUTH MANITOU ISLAND, MICHIGAN
LAKE MICHIGAN
The first lighthouse was established here in 1839. The existing 1872 South Manitou Light tower is the third lighthouse built on the site. The tower and keeper's house sit within Sleeping Bear Dunes National Lakeshore on the southeastern side of the island and overlook the Manitou Passage, an

important shipping channel. The Coast Guard deactivated the station in 1958. Today, the National Park Service maintains the lighthouse, which is open to the public during the summer.

Spectacle Reef Light
NEAR BOIS BLANC ISLAND, MICHIGAN
LAKE HURON
This imposing limestone lighthouse marks treacherous Spectacle Reef along the route to the Straits of Mackinac. It took four years to build the station, but the original ninety-five-foot conical tower has been on station ever since 1874, reinforced a couple of times over the years to protect it from the ever-encroaching ice. The light was automated in 1972. The original second-order Fresnel lens is now on display at the Inland Seas Maritime Museum in Vermilion, Ohio.

Squaw Island Light
NEAR BEAVER ISLAND, MICHIGAN
LAKE MICHIGAN
Located on remote Squaw Island, forty-two miles west of the Mackinac Bridge and five miles north of Beaver Island, this once-handsome red-brick lighthouse, featuring an attached keeper's house with a high-gabled roof and an octagonal tower, was established in 1892. Squaw Island Light was deactivated in 1928. The island is private property, and the lighthouse is not accessible to the public.

St. Clair Flats South Channel Front and Rear Range Lights
NEAR HARSENS ISLAND, MICHIGAN
LAKE ST. CLAIR
The 1859 Front Range Light at the St. Clair Flats, rebuilt in 1875, remains active, though its tower has developed a rather pronounced lean. The Rear Range Light was deactivated in 1907 and now stands in ruins. The SOS Channel Lights Association is working to restore both lights.

St. Helena Island Light
ST. HELENA ISLAND, MICHIGAN
LAKE MICHIGAN
The 1873 St. Helena Island Light sits on the north side of the island, a mile south of the Upper Peninsula shore and six miles west of the Mackinac Bridge. The Great Lakes Lighthouse Keepers Association and the Boy Scouts are in the process of restoring the brick tower and the attached two-story, red-brick keeper's house.

St. James Harbor (Beaver Island Harbor) Light
BEAVER ISLAND, MICHIGAN
LAKE MICHIGAN
The original tower, built in 1852 on the northern side of the island near St. James, lasted only six years before it was

replaced in 1858 by the current cylindrical brick tower. The lighthouse was automated in 1927. Ferries run between St. James and Charlevoix year-round.

St. Joseph North Pier Lights
ST. JOSEPH, MICHIGAN
LAKE MICHIGAN

The first lighthouse at the mouth of the St. Joseph River was built on top of a bluff in 1832. The first pier light at the site was built in 1846. The two existing St. Joseph North Pier Lights, connected by an elevated catwalk, were both built in 1907 and remain active. The Inner Light uses a fifth-order Fresnel lens; the Outer Light uses a fourth-order.

St. Martin Island Light
ST. MARTIN ISLAND, MICHIGAN
LAKE MICHIGAN

The seventy-seven-foot St. Martin Island Light, established in 1905, looks a little odd—given its exoskeleton of six steel posts that rise straight up to support the lantern room. The 1905 fourth-order Fresnel lens and the original clockwork turning mechanism remain in the tower. The keeper's house and a fog signal building stand nearby.

Stannard Rock Light
NEAR MARQUETTE, MICHIGAN
LAKE SUPERIOR

A day beacon marked Stannard Rock, a marine hazard located fifty-five miles north of Marquette and twenty-four miles from the Upper Peninsula shore, from 1868 until the lighthouse was built in 1882. The 102-foot-tall granite tower stands on a crib in eleven feet of water; it took five years to build. After a huge explosion gutted the interior of the station and killed a Coast Guardsman in 1961, the lighthouse was automated. Those who manned this remote station called it the "Loneliest Place in the World."

Sturgeon Point Light
NEAR HARRISVILLE, MICHIGAN
LAKE HURON

Established in 1869, the Sturgeon Point Light is a pretty white station with red trim that is open to the public. The Alcona Historical Society runs a museum in the keeper's house and a gift shop in a building behind the lighthouse.

Tawas Point Light
TAWAS CITY, MICHIGAN
LAKE HURON

The original 1853 light was built on Ottawa Point (later renamed Tawas Point), but over time, waves forced the peninsula to grow farther out into the lake, leaving the tower too far inland. The current tower replaced the landlocked light in 1869. The tower stands within Tawas Point State Park, but it is not open to the public. Visitors may walk the grounds

The Lighthouse Board established the White River Light in 1876 to mark the White River Channel. The government cut the channel between White Lake and Lake Michigan in 1870.

and look out on the stunning blue and green waters of Lake Huron and Tawas Bay from the nearby point.

Thunder Bay Island Light
THUNDER BAY ISLAND, MICHIGAN
LAKE HURON

Built in 1832, the brick tower on Thunder Bay Island off Alpena was heightened in 1857. In 1868, a brick keeper's house was added to the station. Today, a large crack snakes down the side of the tower that faces the lake and the keeper's house is boarded up, but the site remains active and is undergoing restoration.

Waugoshance Light
NEAR WAUGOSHANCE ISLAND, MICHIGAN
LAKE MICHIGAN

Waugoshance Shoal, a dangerous series of reefs and islands seventeen miles west of the Mackinac Bridge, was the site of the first Great Lakes lightship in 1832. The existing lighthouse, built in 1851, was the first of a series of Great Lakes offshore lighthouses to be constructed on cribs. The dilapidated brick lighthouse with a birdcage-style lantern room was deactivated in 1912.

White River Light
WHITEHALL, MICHIGAN
LAKE MICHIGAN

Established in 1876, The White River Light is a pretty station in a rural corner of Michigan. The lighthouse is now a museum open to the public. The third-order Fresnel lens is on display in the gift shop; it was removed from the tower in 1975 after a vandal shot holes in the lantern room and chipped the lens. The lighthouse is rumored to be haunted by the ghosts of the first keeper, Captain William Robinson, and his wife Sarah, who both died at the lighthouse.

White Shoal Light
NEAR WAUGOSHANCE ISLAND, MICHIGAN
LAKE MICHIGAN

As early as 1878, the Chicago Lumbering Company anchored an old schooner twenty miles east of the Mackinac Bridge at White Shoal to mark the dangerous outcropping; it wasn't until 1891 that an official lightship was stationed at the shoal. The current conical steel-and-concrete tower, built in 1910, is the only lighthouse on the Great Lakes that is candy-striped in red and white.

Whitefish Point Light
NEAR PARADISE, MICHIGAN
LAKE SUPERIOR

The original light at Whitefish Point and the light station at Copper Harbor, both established in 1849, were the first light stations built on Lake Superior. Whitefish Point's current skeletal steel tower with a cylindrical central column was erected in 1861. The site remains active and is the home of the Great Lakes Shipwreck Museum.

William Livingstone Memorial Light
DETROIT, MICHIGAN
DETROIT RIVER

This light, established in 1929, was built in honor of William Livingstone, president of the Lake Carriers Association from 1902 until 1925. The marble lighthouse sits on the northern side of Belle Isle, a Detroit city park.

Windmill Point Light
DETROIT, MICHIGAN
DETROIT RIVER

The Windmill Point Light that currently stands in Detroit's Mariners Park was built in 1933 and is the fifth lighthouse to be built on the site. The small, conical, steel-plated tower is whitewashed and supports a modern optic.

Illinois

Calumet Harbor Breakwater South End Light
CALUMET, ILLINOIS
LAKE MICHIGAN

For a distant view of this light, which was established in 1853, visit Calumet Park. The skeletal steel structure with a two-story watchroom lacks a lantern room. A small modern optic still guides vessels in this area of southern Lake Michigan.

Chicago Harbor Light
CHICAGO, ILLINOIS
LAKE MICHIGAN

The first lighthouse at Chicago collapsed only a few hours after it was completed in 1831, delaying the establishment of a lighthouse at Chicago until 1832. The existing light was built at the mouth of the Chicago River in 1893. In 1917, Chicago Harbor Light was moved to its present location on a detached breakwater in the harbor.

Chicago Harbor Southeast Guidewall Light
CHICAGO, ILLINOIS
LAKE MICHIGAN

The Chicago Harbor Southeast Guidewall Light, established just south of Navy Pier in downtown Chicago in 1938, guides vessels through the lock at the mouth of the Chicago River.

Grosse Point Light
EVANSTON, ILLINOIS
LAKE MICHIGAN

The spectacular Grosse Point Light, established in 1874 on the edge of the Northwestern University campus in Evanston remains active and houses a city-run museum. The lighthouse was deactivated during World War II under the National Air Raid Protection Plan and was replaced by lighted buoys seven miles offshore. In 1946, Grosse Point Light was reactivated. The original 1874 second-order Fresnel lens remains in the tower.

Waukegan Harbor Light
WAUKEGAN, ILLINOIS
LAKE MICHIGAN

In 1899, the Waukegan Harbor Light that stands today was built to replace the original light established in 1847. The lighthouse, which houses a modern beacon, remains active. Fire destroyed the lantern room and fog signal in 1967.

Indiana

Buffington Harbor Breakwater Light
GARY, INDIANA
LAKE MICHIGAN

Buffington Harbor Breakwater Light, established in 1926, is located on a breakwater that extends from a private industrial complex, so viewing the light is impossible unless you are on a boat or in a plane. The skinny, faded-red, steel tower remains active at its lonely outpost.

Gary Breakwater Light
GARY, INDIANA
LAKE MICHIGAN

As with the Buffington Harbor Breakwater Light, access to this lighthouse is blocked by an industrial complex. The short, red tower, established in 1911, is not in the best of shape, standing corroded amidst the lake's pounding waves and shifting ice.

Indiana Harbor East Breakwater Light
EAST CHICAGO, INDIANA
LAKE MICHIGAN

Access to the 1935 Indiana Harbor East Breakwater Light, like other lighthouses in this part of northern Indiana, is blocked by an industrial complex. Port Washington Breakwater Light in Wisconsin shares the art deco design of East Breakwater Light and is much easier to view.

Michigan City East Pierhead Light
MICHIGAN CITY, INDIANA
LAKE MICHIGAN

After its construction in 1871, fierce Lake Michigan gales badly battered the Michigan City East Pierhead Light. A particularly nasty storm destroyed the light in 1886; the light was rebuilt. In 1904, it was rebuilt again. The 1904 structure still stands today, connected to shore by a long catwalk stretching along the breakwater to the active station. The light, located at the mouth of Trail Creek in Michigan City, took over the navigational aid duties from the Old Michigan City Light upriver.

Old Michigan City Light
MICHIGAN CITY, INDIANA
LAKE MICHIGAN

Though dark for nearly a century, the Old Michigan City Light still stands, in great shape, on the banks of Trail Creek in Michigan City's Washington Park. The present lighthouse was built in 1858 to replace an earlier lighthouse established on the site in 1837. For forty-three years, Old Michigan City Light was home to the famous lightkeeper Harriet Colfax. When the station was deactivated in 1904, the lantern room and tower on the roof were removed. In 1973, replicas of the tower and lantern room were returned to the roof of the keeper's house. The Michigan City Historical Society now runs a museum in the lighthouse.

Ohio

Ashtabula Light
ASHTABULA, OHIO
LAKE ERIE

The current Ashtabula Light was built in 1905 to replace two lights established at the harbor in 1836. In 1916, the light was moved to its present location on a detached breakwater. A two-day storm in January 1928 encased the station in five feet of ice, sealing the keepers inside. The keepers survived. From the town of Ashtabula, visitors can see the lighthouse in the distance. Ashtabula, where the former keeper's house stands, is also home to the Great Lakes Marine and U.S. Coast Guard Museum.

Cleveland East Pierhead Light
CLEVELAND, OHIO
LAKE ERIE

From a pier behind the Rock and Roll Hall of Fame in downtown Cleveland, visitors can see the two lighthouses in Cleveland Harbor. The East Pierhead Light, established in 1911, is a short, conical cast-iron tower on a detached breakwater.

Cleveland West Breakwater Light
CLEVELAND, OHIO
LAKE ERIE

The Cleveland West Breakwater Light, established in 1911, sits in Cleveland Harbor just across from the East Pierhead Light. The western light has an attached keeper's house.

Conneaut West Breakwater Light
CONNEAUT, OHIO
LAKE ERIE

The art deco Conneaut West Breakwater Light, established in 1936, is very similar in design to the Port Washington Light in Wisconsin. The station never had a lantern room, just an automated beacon on top of the tower. The tower sits at the end of a rough breakwater, which is walkable in fair weather.

Fairport Harbor West Breakwater Light
FAIRPORT HARBOR, OHIO
LAKE ERIE

The lighthouse sits on a breakwater on the west side of the Grand River at Fairport Harbor, across from the Old Fairport Main Light. When Fairport Harbor West Breakwater Light was activated in 1925, the Old Fairport Main Light was extinguished. Headlands Beach State Park provides access to the breakwater, but the lighthouse itself is not open to the public.

Green Island Light
GREEN ISLAND, OHIO
LAKE ERIE

The original Green Island Light, a wooden lighthouse built in 1855, was destroyed in an 1863 fire. A new lighthouse was built at the site two years later. The lighthouse was automated in 1926 and eventually was replaced by a light on a steel tower. In 1939, the Green Island Light was deactivated.

The old, abandoned lighthouse later burned in a blaze started by vandals, and today the station stands in ruins. The island is private property.

Huron Harbor Pierhead Light
HURON, OHIO
LAKE ERIE

The first light at the mouth of the Huron River was built in 1835, but a gale in 1854 destroyed the wooden structure. The iron replacement light was built in 1857. It lit the area until the current art deco light was built in 1939, the same time the pier at the mouth of the Huron River was extended.

Lorain East Breakwater Light
LORAIN, OHIO
LAKE ERIE

This square steel tower, built in 1965, replaced the 1917 light on the opposite breakwater.

Lorain West Breakwater Light
LORAIN, OHIO
LAKE ERIE

A square tower rises from the red-tiled roof of the white-with-green-trim two-story keeper's house. The existing station, built in 1917 to replace the original lighthouse established at this site in 1836, was deactivated in 1966 after the construction of the Lorain East Breakwater Light. When the Coast Guard announced plans to demolish this station, a local movement fought to preserve the lighthouse. The Coast Guard abandoned its plans.

Marblehead Light
MARBLEHEAD, OHIO
LAKE ERIE

The 1821 Marblehead Light—the oldest lighthouse in continuous operation on the Great Lakes—sits at the tip of Marblehead Peninsula in Marblehead Lighthouse State Park near Sandusky. The white stucco light tower and nearby keeper's house, surrounded by a picket fence, is one of the prettiest light stations on the lakes.

Old Fairport Main (Grand River) Light
FAIRPORT HARBOR, OHIO
LAKE ERIE

The sandstone tower and red-brick keeper's house, established in 1825, sit on a hill overlooking Fairport Harbor. The station, rebuilt in 1871, was deactivated in 1925 when the Fairport Harbor West Breakwater Light was established. Today, the lighthouse is home to the Marine Museum, which contains displays of maritime artifacts, the original third-order Fresnel lens from the tower, and a pilothouse from the lake carrier *Frontenac*. The tower is open to the public.

Old Port Clinton Light
PORT CLINTON, OHIO
LAKE ERIE

The Old Port Clinton Light was originally established in 1900 on the other side of the Portage River. After the light was deactivated, the upper half of the light tower was moved across the waterway to the grounds of a private marina.

Sandusky Harbor Pierhead (Cedar Point) Light
SANDUSKY, OHIO
LAKE ERIE

The existing rusty skeletal steel tower of the Sandusky Harbor Pierhead Light was built in 1935. The active light sits near Cedar Point Amusement Park across the bay from the Marblehead Peninsula.

South Bass Island Light
SOUTH BASS ISLAND, OHIO
LAKE ERIE

The lighthouse on the southwestern tip of South Bass Island, established in 1897, was deactivated and replaced by a nearby skeletal steel light in 1962. The lighthouse, owned by the Ohio State University, is not open to the public. For a nice view of the station, take a ferry between the island and the mainland.

Toledo Harbor Light
TOLEDO, OHIO
LAKE ERIE

Toledo Harbor Light is one of the most unusual lights on the Great Lakes. The Romanesque-style light features a buff-colored brick dwelling topped with a rounded eaved roof. The active station is located eight miles off Toledo in Maumee Bay. When Toledo Harbor Light was built in 1904, the nearby Turtle Island Light was darkened.

Turtle Island Light
TURTLE ISLAND, OHIO
LAKE ERIE

The dilapidated tower without its lantern room is all that remains of the Turtle Island Light, established four and one-half miles northeast of Toledo. When the Toledo Harbor Light was built in 1904, Turtle Island Light was deactivated and abandoned. In 1965, a tornado ripped the lantern room from the tower.

Vermilion Light
VERMILION, OHIO
LAKE ERIE

Vermilion Light was first established at this site in 1847 and rebuilt three times. The lighthouse that stands here today, built in 1991, is a replica of the 1877 lighthouse, which was deactivated and removed from the site in 1929. Next to the replica is the Inland Seas Maritime Museum and the research library for the Great Lakes Historical Society.

West Sister Island Light
WEST SISTER ISLAND, OHIO
LAKE ERIE

The West Sister Island Light, established in 1848, stands on the southwestern side of the island, nine miles north of Locust Point in western Lake Erie. The station includes the original tower, but the lantern room has been replaced with a modern optic.

Pennsylvania

Erie Land Light
ERIE, PENNSYLVANIA
LAKE ERIE

When it was lit for the first time in 1819, the Erie Land Light was known as the Presque Isle Light. The Erie Land Light and the Buffalo Main Light are the oldest American lighthouses on the Great Lakes. The Erie Land Light was rebuilt twice and deactivated in 1880, only to be relit in 1885 for fourteen more years of service. Today, the old sandstone light tower, with its replica lantern room, sits in a city park. From the grounds you can see the Erie Pierhead Light on the other side of the bay.

Erie Pierhead Light
PRESQUE ISLE STATE PARK, PENNSYLVANIA
LAKE ERIE

Established in 1927 on the breakwater at the tip of the Presque Isle Peninsula, the Erie Pierhead Light features a square, tapering white tower with a wide black band around its midsection. The lighthouse remains active, guiding vessels in to and out of Presque Isle Bay.

Presque Isle Light
PRESQUE ISLE STATE PARK, PENNSYLVANIA
LAKE ERIE

When this station was established on the lake side of Presque Isle Peninsula in 1873, it adopted the name Presque Isle Light; the light by the same name in Erie was then renamed the Erie Land Light. In 1896, the square white tower of the Presque Isle Light was raised seventeen feet. Today, the attached red-brick keeper's house is home to the manager of Presque Isle State Park and is private property. From the beach in front of the station, visitors can get a closeup view of the active lighthouse.

New York

Barcelona Light
BARCELONA, NEW YORK
LAKE ERIE

The rough stone lighthouse at Barcelona, established in 1829, was the first lighthouse in the world lit by natural gas. After a railroad link was established in nearby Westfield in 1852, ship traffic declined in Barcelona Harbor. The lighthouse was deactivated in 1859. The lighthouse and keeper's house are private property. For a view of the pretty station, travel along Route 5 or go to the marina below the tower.

Braddock Point Light
HILTON, NEW YORK
LAKE ONTARIO

The 1829 Cleveland Light was the inspiration for Braddock Point Light, which was established eleven miles northwest of Rochester in 1896. The Cleveland Light was torn down in 1895, and the station's brass lantern room, Fresnel lens, and other materials were used a year later to build the lighthouse that still stands on this site. After the station was deactivated in 1954, the Coast Guard removed the upper two-thirds of the 110-foot tower due to structural damage. Private owners with an eye for historical accuracy later rebuilt the tower to a height of fifty-five feet and restored the Victorian keeper's house.

Buffalo Breakwater Light
BUFFALO, NEW YORK
LAKE ERIE

After the 1872 Buffalo Breakwater Light was rammed by the freighter *Frontenac* in 1958, the light had a pronounced tilt and quickly earned the nickname of the Buffalo Leaning Lighthouse. Three years later, the octagonal steel tower that now stands replaced the leaning lighthouse, and the old structure was torn down.

Buffalo Breakwater (Old Bottle) Light
BUFFALO, NEW YORK
LAKE ERIE

The cast-iron, Chianti-bottle-shaped Buffalo Breakwater Light, established in 1903, once stood with a sister bottle light on a breakwater in the harbor. After these lights were deactivated in 1985, this light was moved to the Buffalo Coast Guard Station grounds near the Buffalo Main Light. The other bottle light was moved to the grounds of the Dunkirk Light.

Buffalo Main Light
BUFFALO, NEW YORK
LAKE ERIE

When it was lit for the first time in 1819, the Buffalo Main

Light and the Erie Land Light were the first two American lighthouses on the Great Lakes. The tower, rebuilt in 1833, still stands today on the Buffalo Coast Guard Station grounds at the mouth of the Erie Canal and Buffalo River. The lighthouse was deactivated in 1914, but the grounds are open to the public.

Cape Vincent Breakwater Light
CAPE VINCENT, NEW YORK
ST. LAWRENCE RIVER

This short, square lighthouse, established in 1900 and deactivated in 1934, stood on a breakwater in the river until 1951. In the 1950s, the town of Cape Vincent moved the lighthouse to the town hall grounds, well away from the water along NY 12E. Cape Vincent Breakwater Light stands there today, welcoming visitors to this picturesque town.

Charlotte-Genesee Light
ROCHESTER, NEW YORK
LAKE ONTARIO

One of the oldest, prettiest lighthouses on the Great Lakes stands near the mouth of the Genesee River in Charlotte, a once-independent town which is now a section of Rochester. The 1822 sandstone tower and 1863 red-brick keeper's house were deactivated in 1881 and today house a museum and gift shop operated by the Charlotte-Genesee Lighthouse Historical Museum. A fourth-order Fresnel lens, originally from the lighthouse at Lorain, Ohio, is in the tower's replica lantern room.

Crossover Island Light
NEAR CHIPPEWA BAY, NEW YORK
ST. LAWRENCE RIVER

This station was established in 1848 on an island in the St. Lawrence Seaway; it marks the spot where vessels "cross over" between the American and the Canadian channels in the river. The tiny, privately owned island supports a small conical tower and red keeper's house. Crossover Island Light was deactivated in 1941.

Dunkirk Light
DUNKIRK, NEW YORK
LAKE ERIE

The original 1826 lighthouse at Dunkirk burned down and was replaced by the present station in 1875. The keeper's house includes a museum of lighthouse and military history. The tower, which is open to the public, has a Fresnel lens in the lantern room. The second bottle light from Buffalo Harbor, sister to the one near the Buffalo Main Light, is on the grounds along with a light tower that stood on a pier in Dunkirk Harbor from 1939 until 1992.

East Charity Shoal Light
NEAR CAPE VINCENT, NEW YORK
LAKE ONTARIO

The lighthouse tower at East Charity Shoal, located about six miles off Cape Vincent, was built in Vermilion, Ohio, in 1877. In 1929, the Vermilion Light was moved to Buffalo for repairs. Once ready for service in 1935, unbeknownst to the residents of Vermilion, the lighthouse was transferred to a new concrete crib built on East Charity Shoal. You can get a distant view of this station from the grounds of the Tibbets Point Light.

Fort Niagara Light
YOUNGSTOWN, NEW YORK
NIAGARA RIVER

In 1781, the British hoisted the first lighthouse beacon on the Great Lakes into a tower on the roof of Fort Niagara. The current limestone tower was built in 1872 and raised about twenty feet in 1900. Fort Niagara Light was deactivated in 1993. Today, the tower is part of Old Fort Niagara State Park north of Niagara Falls.

Galloo Island Light
GALLOO ISLAND, NEW YORK
LAKE ONTARIO

The Galloo Island Light, established in 1820, was the first American lighthouse built on Lake Ontario. This light tower was shortened in 1867. The tower and attached keeper's house, located about fifteen miles due west of Sackets Harbor, is neglected but still active.

Grand Island Old Front Range Light
GRAND ISLAND, NEW YORK
NIAGARA RIVER

The white-sided wooden tower of the Grand Island Old Front Range Light was established in 1917. It stands on the Buffalo Launch Club grounds, a private marina on the western side of the island, which is located north of Buffalo.

Horseshoe Reef Light
BUFFALO, NEW YORK
LAKE ERIE

The dilapidated Horseshoe Reef Light in Buffalo Harbor can be seen from the grounds of the Buffalo Main Light. The lighthouse was built in Canadian waters in 1856, but when the geographical borders shifted in 1913, the lighthouse found itself in the United States. Horseshoe Reef Light was deactivated in 1920.

Ogdensburg Harbor Light
OGDENSBURG, NEW YORK
ST. LAWRENCE RIVER

The Ogdensburg Harbor Light, established in 1834, is a

private residence but you can get a nice view of the lighthouse from a park on the other side of the Oswegatchie River. The limestone tower rises from the attached keeper's house on Lighthouse Point, just across the river from Prescott, Ontario, and its lighthouses. The Ogdensburg Harbor Light is no longer active.

Oswego West Pierhead Light
OSWEGO, NEW YORK
LAKE ONTARIO

The current light at Oswego, built in 1934, is the last of five lighthouses to be built at the mouth of the Oswego River. In 1942, six Coast Guardsmen were killed at this station when their boat was smashed against the lighthouse's concrete crib.

Rochester Harbor Light
ROCHESTER, NEW YORK
LAKE ONTARIO

The current Rochester Harbor Light that stands today is a steel cylinder dating back only to 1995. After replacing the Charlotte-Genesee Light in 1881, the Rochester Harbor Light has stood on several pierheads in several incarnations.

Rock Island Light
NEAR FISHERS LANDING, NEW YORK
ST. LAWRENCE RIVER

The original tower at Rock Island still stands—it's just a little taller than when it was first built in mid 1847. The conical tower was raised in 1882, and today you can clearly see the two separately constructed sections of the deactivated tower sitting one on top of the other. Rock Island Light was deactivated in 1958, but the State of New York owns Rock Island and maintains it as a park.

Sackets Harbor (Horse Island) Light
HORSE ISLAND, NEW YORK
LAKE ONTARIO

You can get a distant view of this light while onshore at Sackets Harbor Battlefield State Park. The existing lighthouse, built in 1870 to replace the deteriorating 1831 light, is on private property and off-limits for up-close viewing. Though the old lighthouse was deactivated in 1957, a nearby modern beacon on a skeletal tower guides vessels traveling in to and out of Sackets Harbor.

Selkirk (Salmon River) Light
NEAR PORT ONTARIO, NEW YORK
LAKE ONTARIO

The Selkirk Light, established in 1838, sits at the mouth of the Salmon River about four miles west of Pulaski. The wooden tower, with its birdcage-style lantern room, pokes from the roof of the two-and-a-half-story fieldstone keeper's house. Selkirk (Salmon River) Light was deactivated in 1859.

Sisters Island Light
NEAR CHIPPEWA BAY, NEW YORK
ST. LAWRENCE RIVER

The Sisters Island Light, built of native limestone in 1870, sits well-preserved on the island, facing Canada. The light was deactivated in the 1950s.

Sodus Outer Light
SODUS POINT, NEW YORK
LAKE ONTARIO

The first pier at the entrance to Sodus Bay was built in 1834 with a beacon on the pierhead. A more-permanent beacon was erected in 1870 and rebuilt in 1901. The Old Sodus Light on shore was deactivated, and this lighthouse became the primary lighthouse to mark the entrance to Sodus Bay. The light is still active.

Sodus Point Light
SODUS POINT, NEW YORK
LAKE ONTARIO

The existing Sodus Point Light, built in 1871 to replace an 1825 lighthouse on the site, has been dark since 1901. But today, the limestone tower and attached keeper's house are open to the public. The Sodus Bay Historical Society runs a delightful museum and gift shop at the site.

South Buffalo South Side Light
BUFFALO, NEW YORK
LAKE ERIE

The 1903 South Buffalo South Side Light sits on a lonely peninsula in a private industrial area, three miles south of the Buffalo Main Light. The station, which was deactivated in 1992, is not open to the public, but you can get a look at it from Fuhrmann Boulevard.

Stony Point Light
NEAR HENDERSON HARBOR, NEW YORK
LAKE ONTARIO

The Stony Point Light, with a square tower attached to the front of the keeper's house, resembles the nearby Sackets Harbor (Horse Island) Light. The existing tower was built in 1869 to replace the original lighthouse built in 1830. Today, the privately owned inactive station shows its age.

Sunken Rock Light
ALEXANDRIA BAY, NEW YORK
ST. LAWRENCE RIVER

Sunken Rock Light, a small white lighthouse with a green lantern room, was established in 1847 on a tiny island located in the harbor at Alexandria Bay. Somehow, a storage building also squeezes onto the island.

Thirty Mile Point Light
SOMERSET, NEW YORK
LAKE ONTARIO

The sturdy limestone lighthouse at Thirty Mile Point, built in 1875 and lit for the first time the following year, marks a sand bar that stretches out into the lake from the point. The beacon was removed from the lantern room and placed on a nearby steel tower in 1958, but the tower, keeper's house, and numerous outbuildings are in great shape and are open to the public. Golden Hill State Park campground is right next door.

Tibbetts Point Light
NEAR CAPE VINCENT, NEW YORK
LAKE ONTARIO

The original light at Tibbetts Point was built in 1827, and the white stucco tower that stands there today was erected in 1854. The lighthouse was automated in 1981, but it still houses the 1854 fourth-order Fresnel lens. A small, plastic light on the balcony outside the lantern room serves as the beacon today. Several buildings stand on the lighthouse grounds, including a keeper's house that is now an American Youth Hostel. In another building, the Tibbetts Point Lighthouse Historical Society runs a gift shop. On the horizon west of Tibbetts Point, the East Charity Shoal Light is just visible.

Ontario

Battle Island Light
BATTLE ISLAND, ONTARIO
LAKE SUPERIOR

This remote light, established in 1877, stands on top of a cliff on the northern shore of Lake Superior, about seven miles south of Rossport. The nearby duplex once housed a head keeper and an assistant. Automated in 1991, the Battle Island Light was the last Great Lakes station to have an official lightkeeper.

Bellevue Park Old Range Light
SAULT STE. MARIE, ONTARIO
ST. MARY'S RIVER

The Bellevue Park Old Range Light is located in the park on Topsail Island east of the Soo Locks. The wooden, white-with-black-trim range light is no longer active, and the lantern room at the top of the pyramidal tower is boarded up.

Big Tub (Lighthouse Point) Light
TOBERMORY, ONTARIO
LAKE HURON

The first light, established in 1881 on Big Tub Harbour near Tobermory at the tip of the Bruce Peninsula in western Lake Huron, was simply a hanging lantern. The six-sided wooden tower with cedar shingles that stands today was built in 1885.

Bois Blanc (Boblo) Island Light
BOIS BLANC (BOBLO) ISLAND, ONTARIO
DETROIT RIVER

Bois Blanc (Boblo) Island, located in the Detroit River near where it unites with Lake Erie, has harbored a lighthouse on its southern tip since 1839. Today, the conical stone tower sans lantern room stands in ruins.

Brebeuf Island Front Range and Beausoleil Island Rear Range Lights
BREBEUF ISLAND AND BEAUSOLEIL ISLAND, ONTARIO
LAKE HURON

These range lights sit about a quarter of a mile apart on separate islands in the southeastern corner of Georgian Bay. The front range light on Brebeuf Island was established in 1878 on nearby Gin Rock, but was moved to its present location in 1900 to create a range system with the light on Beausoleil Island, which was established that same year. The present Beausoleil Island Rear Range Light was rebuilt in 1915 as a skeletal steel light towering above the treetops of this woodsy island.

Burlington Canal Front Range and Burlington Main Lights
BURLINGTON, ONTARIO
LAKE ONTARIO

The Burlington Canal Front Range Light, established in 1842, and the Burlington Main Light, established in 1837, were once part of a range system marking the Burlington Canal; only the Front Range Light remains active. The original wooden Burlington Main Light was destroyed in a fire in 1856; the existing cylindrical limestone tower was erected in 1858. A red-brick keeper's house is nearby.

Bustard Rocks Main, Inner, and Outer Range Lights
BUSTARD ROCKS, ONTARIO
LAKE HURON

The three range lights on the Bustard Rocks—about three miles south of the mouth of the French River in Georgian Bay in northeastern Lake Huron—were built as part of the French River range system along with the French River Range Lights. The main and inner lights were established in 1875, and the outer light was established in 1893. When these lights were manned, one keeper maintained all five light towers.

Byng Inlet Range Lights
BYNG INLET, ONTARIO
LAKE HURON

These range lights, established in 1890, still guide vessels past the treacherous Magnetawan Ledges and Burton Bank into the town of Byng Inlet on Georgian Bay. Before the lights were automated, they were tended by the keeper of the nearby Gereaux Island Light.

Cabot Head Light
CABOT HEAD, ONTARIO
LAKE HURON

The Cabot Head Light, established in 1896, sits on the north-eastern tip of the Bruce Peninsula on Georgian Bay. The original light tower, which rose from a corner of the keeper's house, was removed in 1971 when the beacon was transferred to a skeletal steel tower. In 1993, the Friends of Cabot Head began restoration work on the station. By 1995, the group had rebuilt the tower and established a museum in the keeper's house.

Cape Croker Light
CAPE CROKER, ONTARIO
LAKE HURON

The 1898 Cape Croker Light was a wooden tower on top of a keeper's house, but that light was replaced by the current tower constructed of reinforced concrete in 1909. The light, located on the Bruce Peninsula in the southern part of Georgian Bay, remains active. A 1958 keeper's house sits nearby.

Caribou Island Light
NEAR CARIBOU ISLAND, ONTARIO
LAKE SUPERIOR

This active Coast Guard station and lighthouse sits on a tiny island just south of the much-larger Caribou Island. In 1912, the current eighty-two-foot hexagonal tower of reinforced concrete supported by flying buttresses replaced the 1886 station. Several outbuildings, a pier, and a helipad complete this compact, tidy station.

Chantry Island Light
CHANTRY ISLAND, ONTARIO
LAKE HURON

The whitewashed, limestone tower on the eastern side of Chantry Island off Southampton, established in 1859, is one of six "Imperial Towers" built around the Bruce Peninsula in the mid 1800s. The eighty-six-foot light tower is in good condition and remains active. The keeper's house, however, stands in ruins nearby.

Christian Island Light
CHRISTIAN ISLAND, ONTARIO
LAKE HURON

The whitewashed, limestone tower on the southern end of Christian Island, established in 1859, is one of six "Imperial Towers" built around the Bruce Peninsula in the mid 1800s. The lantern room was removed and cut up for scrap during World War II, and today this tower supports a modern beacon. The ruins of a limestone keeper's house are nearby.

Colchester Reef Light
NEAR COLCHESTER, ONTARIO
LAKE ERIE

In the 1870s, a lightship was stationed over this dangerous reef, located about five miles south of Colchester; the lightship sank in an 1883 gale. The sturdier Colchester Reef Light was built two years later. Today, a helipad and a fifteen-foot skeletal steel tower which supports an active beacon sit on top of the lopped-off 1885 stone light tower.

Coppermine Point Light
NEAR BATCHAWANA BAY, ONTARIO
LAKE SUPERIOR

Coppermine Point Light was established in 1910. After it was deactivated in the 1960s, this pyramidal wooden tower was moved to its present location near a restaurant just north of the town of Batchawana Bay.

Corunna Rear Range Light
MOORETOWN, ONTARIO
ST. CLAIR RIVER

The Corunna Rear Range Light was established in 1890 in the town of Corunna on the St. Clair River. When the lighthouse was deactivaed in 1941, the town of Corunna bought it. But in 1951, the Canadian Coast Guard bought it back and put the light back in service. The light shined until 1982 when a taller steel tower replaced it. The town of Corunna once again bought the light and moved it to the Moore Museum in nearby Mooretown, where it stands today.

Cove Island Light
COVE ISLAND, ONTARIO
LAKE HURON

The whitewashed, limestone tower on the northwestern tip of Cove Island off the end of the Bruce Peninsula, established in 1858, is one of six "Imperial Towers" built around the peninsula in the mid 1800s. The light tower sits next to a limestone keeper's house and a small workshop built in 1962. Two other dwellings, a fog signal building, a radio tower, a boathouse, and a helipad complete this large station complex.

Davieaux Island Light
DAVIEAUX ISLAND, ONTARIO
LAKE SUPERIOR

The original Davieaux Island Light was built in 1872 on the southern end of Michipicoten Island in northeastern Lake Superior. In 1911, the original light was replaced by the present hexagonal, reinforced-concrete tower on a small island alongside Michipicoten Island. The island was named in honor of the light station's first keeper, Charles Davieaux.

False Duck Island Light

NEAR SOUTH BAY, ONTARIO

LAKE ONTARIO

The original False Duck Island Light, established in 1829, was deactivated and torn down in 1965 when a modern signal beacon was built. In 1967, however, the balcony, lantern room, and lens from the old tower were placed atop a reproduction stone tower. Today, the reproduction lighthouse is part of the Mariner's Memorial Park and Museum, which pays tribute to the sailors of Prince Edward County who died on Lake Ontario.

French River Front and Rear Range Lights

NEAR BIGWOOD, ONTARIO

LAKE HURON

These two range lights sit three-quarters of a mile apart at the mouth of the French River on Georgian Bay. Both lights were established in 1875 as part of a range system along with the towers on the Bustard Rocks, which stand three miles offshore.

Gereaux Island Light

GEREAUX ISLAND, ONTARIO

LAKE HURON

The rickety original tower established in 1870 on Gereaux Island was active only a few years before the government replaced it with the present station in 1880. The white, pyramidal tower sits on the south side of the entrance to Byng Inlet. A seasonal Coast Guard search-and-rescue station operates out of the station's nearby boathouse.

Gibraltar Point Light

TORONTO, ONTARIO

LAKE ONTARIO

The limestone lighthouse at Gibraltar Point, established in 1808 on Centre Island in Toronto Harbour, is the oldest lighthouse still standing on the Great Lakes. Though deactivated and replaced by a skeletal steel tower in 1958, the historic tower is maintained by the Metro Toronto Parks Board and is in wonderful condition.

Goderich Light

GODERICH, ONTARIO

LAKE HURON

Although the 1847 square masonry Goderich Light is only thirty-five feet tall, the tower stands high on a cliff located south of Goderich Harbor and casts light a considerable distance over Lake Huron.

Great Duck Island Light

GREAT DUCK ISLAND, ONTARIO

LAKE HURON

The original tower and keeper's house were built in 1877 on the southwestern side of Great Duck Island, located twelve miles south of Manitoulin Island in northern Lake Huron. The taller existing tower replaced the original light in 1918. In 1995, the Canadian Coast Guard demolished the keeper's house.

Griffith Island Light

GRIFFITH ISLAND, ONTARIO

LAKE HURON

The whitewashed, limestone tower established on the eastern side of Griffith Island in 1858 is one of six "Imperial Towers" built around the Bruce Peninsula in the mid 1800s. The fifty-five-foot tower is in very good shape, but the nearby limestone keeper's house is in ruins.

Gros Cap Reef Light

NEAR GROS CAP, ONTARIO

LAKE SUPERIOR

The plow-shaped concrete crib which supports this modern light station is designed to divert encroaching ice flows and storm surges. Above the crib, a two-story building supports a helipad and a towering red-and-white radio antenna. When this station was established in 1962, it made the American light at Point Iroquois, Michigan, obsolete.

Hope Island Light

HOPE ISLAND, ONTARIO

LAKE HURON

These days, the old lighthouse, established in 1884 on the northern tip of Hope Island in southern Georgian Bay, looks a little rundown and lacks a lantern room. In the 1990s, a light on a skeletal tower replaced the original beacon.

Ile Parisienne Light

ILE PARISIENNE, ONTARIO

LAKE SUPERIOR

This petite tower, located just north of the Soo Locks on the southwestern side of Ile Parisienne, sees a lot of shipping traffic. Established in 1912, the whitewashed tower is made of reinforced concrete and has a bright-red lantern room. A keeper's house and two other buildings stand nearby.

Janet Head (Gore Bay) Light

NEAR GORE BAY, ONTARIO

LAKE HURON

This white-with-red-trim wooden tower and attached keeper's house, established in 1879, stands on a point near the town of Gore Bay on Manitoulin Island.

Jones Island and Gordon Rocks Range Lights

JONES ISLAND AND GORDON ROCKS, ONTARIO

LAKE HURON

These two range lights, established in 1894, help guide ships into Parry Sound off Georgian Bay. The Front Range Light on desolate Jones Island rises from the center of a red-roofed keeper's house. The companion Rear Range Light tower stands alone at the highest point on the Gordon Rocks.

Kagawong Light
KAGAWONG, ONTARIO
LAKE HURON

This active light stands on the north-central side of Lake Huron's Manitoulin Island. The first light was established here in 1880, but was replaced only eight years later by a light on a pole. After a fire destroyed the pole light in 1892, the existing tower was built in 1894.

Killarney East Light
KILLARNEY, ONTARIO
LAKE HURON

The original light tower on this gently sloping rocky point on Georgian Bay was built in 1866. The existing Killarney East Light was built in 1909. When manned, the keeper maintained both the east and the west lights.

Killarney West Light
KILLARNEY, ONTARIO
LAKE HURON

The Killarney West Light, also established in 1866, was rebuilt along with the Killarney East Light in 1909. The square, white, tapered tower is on Partridge Island just west of Killarney.

Kincardine Front and Rear Range Lights
KINCARDINE, ONTARIO
LAKE HURON

This range system, established in 1881, guides vessels up the Penetagore River at the picturesque town of Kincardine. The small Front Range Light is on a pier at the mouth of the river about five hundred yards west of the Rear Range Light. The Rear Range Light consists of a tower poking from the roof of a keeper's house, which is built into the side of a hill. The keeper's house serves as a clubhouse for the Kincardine Yacht Club and a museum.

Kingsville Light
KINGSVILLE, ONTARIO
LAKE ERIE

Once shining its beacon from the lakeshore, the Kingsville Light is now inactive and landlocked on private property in the city of Kingsville. Established in 1889, the light is a little rundown these days, with large swaths of siding missing.

Lion's Head Light
LION'S HEAD, ONTARIO
LAKE HURON

In 1903, a light on a pole originally marked Lion's Head on the Bruce Peninsula. The first lighthouse was built here in

1911, only to be rebuilt several times. In 1969, the Canadian Coast Guard finally demolished the station and replaced it with an automated beacon on a pier. In 1983, students at Bruce Peninsula District School designed and rebuilt the lighthouse. The lighthouse that stands today is the result of their efforts.

Lonely Island Light
LONELY ISLAND, ONTARIO
LAKE HURON

This light station, established in 1870 and located ten miles south of Manitoulin Island, originally consisted of a tower attached to a keeper's house. The original lighthouse burned down, and the station, including the still-standing light tower near the center of the island, was rebuilt in 1907. In 1995, the Canadian Coast Guard tore down the 1907 keeper's house and boathouse; a bungalow was added in 1962.

Long Point Light
LONG POINT, ONTARIO
LAKE ERIE

The weather near remote Long Point is particularly wicked. In fact, the first lighthouse established here in 1830 was battered badly enough to warrant replacement only thirteen years after it was built. The present tower, built in 1916, stands within a National Wildlife Area.

Main Duck Island Light
MAIN DUCK ISLAND, ONTARIO
LAKE ONTARIO

The Main Duck Island Light, established in 1914, stands on the north side of the island in northeastern Lake Ontario. The beacon remains active, guiding vessels along the area's high-traffic shipping lanes.

Manitowaning Light
MANITOWANING, ONTARIO
LAKE HURON

This white, wooden tower, established in 1885, stands on a bluff overlooking the Manitoulin Island town of Manitowaning.

McKay Island (Bruce Mines) Light
NEAR BRUCE MINES, ONTARIO
ST. JOSEPH CHANNEL

The 1907 McKay Island Light is no longer active, but a skeletal steel tower located in front of the light shines a modern beacon over the channel.

Meaford Rear Range Light
MEAFORD, ONTARIO
LAKE HURON

The earliest navigational beacon at Meaford was a light atop a wooden frame erected around 1875. The existing

Rear Range Light, a skeletal steel tower bolted to the top of a pumphouse, was built in the first half of the twentieth century to serve as a range light in tandem with the Harbor Breakwater Light. Both of the lights were deactivated in 1988, and the harbor light and breakwater were removed. The pumphouse with its diminutive range light today houses the Meaford Museum.

Michipicoten Island (East End) Light
MICHIPICOTEN ISLAND, ONTARIO
LAKE SUPERIOR
Established on the southeastern side of Michipicoten Island in 1912, this six-sided light tower of white, reinforced concrete is supported by flying buttresses and topped with a round, red lantern room. Several outbuildings surround the tower.

Mississagi Strait Light
NEAR MELDRUM BAY, ONTARIO
LAKE HURON
The Mississagi Strait Light was established on the far western end of Manitoulin Island in 1873. The original station was deactivated in 1968 and now houses a museum. Today, a light on a pole nearby aids vessels moving up the strait.

Mohawk Island Light
MOHAWK ISLAND, ONTARIO
LAKE ERIE
The limestone lighthouse and keeper's house on tiny Mohawk Island were built in 1848 to mark not only the island but also a dangerous reef nearby. The lighthouse, however, lost its importance when the entrance to the Welland Canal shifted farther away from the island. Since deactivation in 1969, the condition of the lighthouse has deteriorated, and today it stands in ruins.

Niagara River Front and Rear Range Lights
NIAGARA-ON-THE-LAKE, ONTARIO
NIAGARA RIVER
In 1903, the Niagara River Range Lights were established where the river meets Lake Ontario. The white towers with red lantern rooms look nearly identical—the only difference is the Rear Range Light is taller.

Nine Mile Point Light
SIMCOE ISLAND, ONTARIO
LAKE ONTARIO
Nine Mile Point Light, established in 1833, is a white roughstone tower with red trim connected to a wooden keeper's house. The lighthouse sits on the western tip of Simcoe Island where the St. Lawrence River flows from Lake Ontario.

Nottawasaga Island Light
NOTTAWASAGA ISLAND, ONTARIO
LAKE HURON
The whitewashed, limestone tower on Nottawasaga Island, located off the town of Collingwood, is one of six "Imperial Towers" built around the Bruce Peninsula in the mid 1800s. A 1959 fire destroyed the attached limestone keeper's house, and today it remains in ruins. The lighthouse was automated after the fire and remains active.

Oakville Light
OAKVILLE, ONTARIO
LAKE ONTARIO
The original Oakville Light, built in 1837, stood on a pierhead in the harbor until 1886 when a particularly vicious storm destroyed the tower. The lighthouse that stands today is the replacement light that was built in 1889. In the 1960s, the lighthouse was deactivated and moved to its present location in Oakville's Shipyard Park.

Old Long Point (Cut) Light
NEAR LONG POINT, ONTARIO
LAKE ERIE
The Old Long Point (Cut) Light, built in 1879, once marked a channel through the Long Point Peninsula. A 1906 storm filled in this natural "cut," and the lighthouse was active for only ten more years. At one point, someone removed the lantern room and replaced it with an enclosed observation deck. Today, the green, square lighthouse and integrated keeper's house is a private residence near Long Point Provincial Park.

Old Pelee Passage Light
WINDSOR, ONTARIO
LAKE ERIE
The Old Pelee Passage Light, built in 1902 to replace the light established here in 1861, was originally stationed between Pelee Island and Point Pelee, about where the present Pelee Passage Light stands today. After the light was deactivated in 1975, it was moved to a new home in Windsor's Lakeview Park.

Otter Island Light
OTTER ISLAND, ONTARIO
LAKE SUPERIOR
This *very* remote lighthouse, established in 1903, sits on Otter Island, located off the shore of Pukaskwa National Park in northeastern Lake Superior. The small, white wooden tower has a keeper's house and a smaller outbuilding nearby.

Pelee Island Light
PELEE ISLAND, ONTARIO
LAKE ERIE

Stripped of its lantern room and windows, the 1833 gray stone tower of the Pelee Island Light is all that remains of this station on the north side of the island. A committee has formed that hopes to restore the abandoned light, which was deactivated in 1909. The island is a major breeding ground for numerous bird species.

Pelee Passage Light
NEAR PELEE ISLAND, ONTARIO
LAKE ERIE

Since 1861, the Pelee Passage Light has marked Middle Ground Shoal, located northeast of Pelee Island. The original lighthouse was replaced in 1902. When the present lighthouse was built in 1975, the 1902 lighthouse was moved to Lakeview Park in Windsor, where it still stands. The 1975 lighthouse consists of a one-story, flat building perched on top of a twenty-foot metal pole that rises from Lake Erie. The roof of the building doubles as a helipad, and in one corner of the roof, a thirty-foot light tower rises to support a green lantern room.

Pigeon Island Light
PIGEON ISLAND, ONTARIO
LAKE ONTARIO

Pigeon Island is a tiny isle in Lake Ontario southwest of Wolfe Island. Pigeon Island Light, which stands at the center of the island, is an active skeletal steel tower. The tower is the only structure on the island.

Point Abino Light
NEAR CRYSTAL BEACH, ONTARIO
LAKE ERIE

Established in 1912, the *Buffalo Lightship* marked the dangerous shoal extending from Point Abino until 1913, when it sank in a vicious November storm. Everyone on board perished. Point Abino Light, a stunning, Greek Revival lighthouse, replaced the lightship in 1917. The light consists of a square, white tower with red accents; it is integrated into the one-story keeper's house. The light was automated in 1988 and deactivated in 1996, but the twelve-sided lantern room still contains a Fresnel lens.

Point Clark Light
POINT CLARK, ONTARIO
LAKE HURON

The whitewashed, limestone tower that stands at Point Clark, located about ten miles south of Kincardine, is one of six "Imperial Towers" built around the Bruce Peninsula in the mid 1800s. A nearby keeper's house harbors a maritime museum, and the active station is now a National Historic Site.

Point Petre Light
NEAR CHERRY VALLEY, ONTARIO
LAKE ONTARIO

The original white masonry tower of the Point Petre Light, built in 1833, stood at the southwestern tip of Quinte Island for 144 years before it was replaced with the present skinny, red-and-white tower of reinforced concrete. Today, the lighthouse stands within a Government Environment Research center, and access to the light is restricted.

Pointe au Baril Range Lights
POINTE AU BARIL, ONTARIO
LAKE HURON

In 1889, area fishermen first put a light inside a barrel to help guide them back in from Georgian Bay in northeastern Lake Huron. That quirky range light led to the naming of this peninsula and town — Pointe au Baril. Today, the Front Range Light is a white pyramidal tower with attached keeper's house. The Rear Range Light is a steel tower on nearby Macklin Island.

Porphyry Point Light
EDWARD ISLAND, ONTARIO
LAKE SUPERIOR

The lighthouse on Porphyry Point, located about thirty miles east of Thunder Bay at the southern tip of Edward Island, includes a forty-eight-foot-tall square light tower enclosed in a skeletal steel support system. Two keeper's houses sit behind the tower, and a fog signal building resides closer to the water. Porphyry Point Light was established in 1873.

Port Burwell and Port Burwell Approach Lights
PORT BURWELL, ONTARIO
LAKE ERIE

The wooden Port Burwell Light on the eastern side of Otter Creek, established in 1840, was deactivated in 1963. In 1986, the town of Port Burwell hired Mennonite craftsmen to extensively renovate the light station. Today, visitors can climb the tower and see the original Fresnel lens in the adjacent maritime museum. The active Port Burwell Approach Light, established in 1963, is on the western pierhead across from the Port Burwell Light.

Port Colborne Inner and Outer Lights
PORT COLBORNE, ONTARIO
LAKE ERIE

Port Colborne and its active range lights sit at the southern terminus of the Welland Canal, which flows between Lakes Erie and Ontario. The original lighthouse at Port Colborne, established in 1834, was replaced twice, as the entrance to the canal shifted. The present Inner Light on the north breakwall was built in 1903. The Outer Light on the south breakwall was built in 1928 to replace an earlier inland range light.

Port Dalhousie Front and Rear Range Lights
PORT DALHOUSIE, ONTARIO
LAKE ONTARIO

These range lights were originally intended to mark the northern end of the Welland Canal, which flowed between Lakes Erie and Ontario and exited at Port Dalhousie. The existing Rear Range Light was erected in 1898 to replace the original light established here in 1852. The present Front Range Light, at the end of a 1,500-foot pier extending from the Rear Range Light, dates to 1879. The rear light was deactivated in 1988.

Port Dover Light
PORT DOVER, ONTARIO
LAKE ERIE

The original 1846 pyramid-shaped wooden tower still stands on the western pierhead at the mouth of the Lynn River at Port Dover. The active station now sports aluminum siding.

Port Maitland Front Range Light
PORT MAITLAND, ONTARIO
LAKE ERIE

This pyramidal white tower, established in 1830, stands on the west pier at the mouth of the Grand River in Port Maitland.

Port Stanley Light
PORT STANLEY, ONTARIO
LAKE ERIE

The pyramidal, white, reinforced-concrete tower was established on the western pierhead at Port Stanley in 1908. It supports an active green beacon.

Port Weller Outer Light
PORT WELLER, ONTARIO
LAKE ONTARIO

The Port Weller Outer Light marks the present northern terminus of the Welland Canal, which runs between Lakes Erie and Ontario, bypassing the falls on the Niagara River. The art deco tower of reinforced concrete, topped with a skeletal steel structure, was established at the end of the west pier in 1931. A matching art deco keeper's house stands on the pier near shore.

Prescott Inner (Rotary) and Outer Harbor Lights
PRESCOTT, ONTARIO
ST. LAWRENCE RIVER

The Prescott Inner and Outer Harbor Lights, established in 1989, stand at the marina in Prescott, directly across the St. Lawrence River from Ogdensburg, New York. The Inner Light is a replica of the original light; it houses a tourist information center and an ice cream shop. The lantern room houses a Fresnel lens donated by the Canadian Coast Guard, and the lighthouse operates as a private aid to navigation. Across the marina from the Inner Light on the end of the marina breakwater, the petite, skinny Outer Light shines its green beacon.

Presqu'ile Point Light
NEAR BRIGHTON, ONTARIO
LAKE ONTARIO

The 1840 Presqu'ile Point Light, which stands within Presqu'ile Provincial Park, supports a small plastic optic; the lantern room was removed after the light was automated in 1952. The keeper's house contains a natural history museum.

Prince Edward Point (Point Traverse) Light
NEAR SOUTH BAY, ONTARIO
LAKE ONTARIO

The pyramidal tower and two-story keeper's house of the original lighthouse, built in 1881, sit near the skeletal steel tower that replaced this beacon. The Prince Edward Point Light's lantern room was removed when the light was deactivated in 1959. The wooden tower stands today decapitated and desheveled on the southeastern end of Quinte Island.

Queen's Wharf Light
TORONTO, ONTARIO
LAKE ONTARIO

The original lighthouse on Queen's Wharf in Toronto Harbour was built in 1838, but it was replaced by a range system in 1861. The range lights remained active until 1911 when they were deactivated and abandoned. In 1929, one of the range lights was moved to its present location in downtown Toronto about a half mile from the harbor. The other range light no longer stands.

Red Rock Light
RED ROCK ISLAND, ONTARIO
LAKE HURON

A storm destroyed the original 1870 wooden light on nearby Old Tower Island, and in 1881 a wooden light was built on Red Rock Island at the entrance to Parry Sound in Georgian Bay to replace it. But the replacement light couldn't withstand the storms either, and in 1911 the present squat cylindrical tower was built. In the early 1970s, a helipad was erected above the lantern room, giving the station the look of a lighthouse on graduation day.

Rondeau East and West Pierhead Lights
ERIEAU, ONTARIO
LAKE ERIE

The skeletal East Pierhead Light and the pyramidal West Pierhead Light are also known as the Erieau East and West Pierhead Lights. The lights mark the entrance to Rondeau Harbor.

Index

About the Author and Photographer

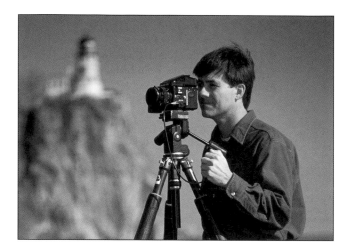

Photograph copyright Denise Dempster.

Photograph copyright Tim Berger.

Daniel Dempster has been a professional photographer since 1989. His images of lighthouses, landscapes, equines, canines and many other subjects have graced the pages of many calendars, books, and publications, including *Audubon*, *Smithsonian*, *McCalls*, *Reader's Digest*, Voyageur Press, and Brown Trout. He was the official photographer for the Kentucky Derby Festival for twelve years, and in 1993 he won two International Festival Association gold awards. His work encompasses all of his many interests, and he spends much of his time making images of subjects that intrigue him. Daniel and his wife have shared an interest in lighthouses for many years, and they photograph them any time they are near the waters of the Great Lakes or the oceans' shores.

Daniel makes his home in the rolling hills of southern Indiana with his wife, Denise, his two children, Jason and Julia, and their three dogs and three cats.

Author Todd R. Berger traveled more than 8,000 miles in a Honda Civic while writing *Lighthouses of the Great Lakes*. He is the editor of dozens of photographic books on travel throughout the Midwest, Pacific Northwest, Southeast, and New England, and the editor of eleven anthologies on subjects ranging from dogs to outdoor sports. He is a freelance writer and editor based in Saint Paul, Minnesota.